R. Buckminster Fuller

R. Buckminster Fuller
by John McHale

George Braziller New York 1962

Contents

World architecture, in the unitary sense employed today, is a phenomenon of quite recent origin. Increased speed of communication in the 20th century has made it possible for the architect or engineer to operate in world terms. He is called upon to build in far-flung locations to the requirements of different climatic and social conditions. His works may also be known on a world-wide scale as never before, for ideas and styles now move swiftly around the earth and are rapidly diffused throughout diverse cultures and environments. This acceleration in communication, however, is but one facet of the vast technological revolution which has long been transforming not only our society but the physical environment within which that society functions.

This transforming agency has been the direct application of science through industrial technology to human affairs. For the first time in history, man possesses the potential means to satisfy living requirements to the fullest extent, not only for the few but for all men. In translating the context of architecture, from a local to a global scale, this agency of change has also enlarged the role and widened the responsibility of the architect. He no longer serves only the needs of his immediate community within the limits of local materials, techniques, and knowledge; he may also deal with the requirements of a whole society through the relatively unlimited potential of these industrialized means. The full measure, therefore, of a truly "world" architecture must be gauged not only by the fortuitous global distribution of individual masterworks or the width of their stylistic influence, but also by the extent to which it embraces the challenge and responsibility implied in the technological basis of an emergent world society.

The work of Buckminster Fuller pre-eminently can be judged by the latter criterion. His first sketch was of a "one world" town plan (plate 1). His first detailed project of a house—designed for mass production, yet embodying the highest living standards available—was planned for use in any part of the world and was capable of being delivered by air to even the most remote location (plates 2–5). The central theme of his third-of-a-century pioneer exploration has been one of dedication to the idea of a world-wide "architec-

10   tural" or "shelter" facility as part of the scientifically designed investment of total world resources in the service of all
humanity.

This monograph is largely a record of external activities
belonging in the public domain. In a lifetime of arduous,
self-initiated exploration (often conducted in isolation and
in the face of many checks and reverses), the internal dia-
logues which accompanied and energized these external events
may well be the more fascinating aspect of a rare adventure
of the human spirit. Clarification of them, however, must be
left to the future.

By considering, initially, early influences and the events of Fuller's formative years, we may gain some insight into the radical nature of his thought. He was born in 1895, in Milton, Massachusetts, on that part of the American seaboard which faces Europe and which has functioned historically as an entrance to the New World. His family, New Englanders since 1632, have always played a continuing role of public service. Until the father of Buckminster Fuller broke family precedent by becoming a merchant, each generation of the family had been engaged in the ministry, letters, or law. Important among its many distinguished members were the Honorable Timothy Fuller, an early 18th-century Speaker of the Massachusetts House of Representatives, and his daughter, Margaret Fuller, an ardent feminist and woman of letters, founder and editor of *The Dial*,[1] literary editor for the New York *Herald Tribune*, and translator of Goethe and Schiller.

Fuller's early years within such a family tradition, fusing strains of romantic idealism with practical interests and action in community affairs, must have given him a particular sense of continuity with the past. This may seem paradoxical in relation to his mature work which is so uncompromisingly oriented toward the future; but the unfettered quality of his ideas may well proceed from the security of a creative, individualistic family. Fuller has never felt cut off from his historical antecedents, a factor which so often shackles the contemporary imagination.

Fuller attributes his first design stimulations to boyhood summers spent on a small island in Penobscot Bay off the coast of Maine. "Boatbuilding was the parent technology. . . . Fishing the local industry, and such tension systems as seines, trawls, weirs, scallop drags, lobster-pot heads, and traps, together with all their respective drag and buoy gear, insured an ever-present abundance of stout cordage and light lines as well as experience in net weaving, tieing, splicing and serving. Here men 'passed a line' and 'took turn' in deft tension techniques as spontaneous as those of spiders." According to Fuller, "We had in our sloop one of the earliest auxiliary gasoline engines within a many-mile radius, and this induced a whole line of inventiveness, along with gallons

12 of sweat, relevant to priming the engine, testing the spark, and rolling over a flywheel."[2]

Formal schooling led, in the family tradition, to Harvard in 1913, but Fuller's disinclination for orthodox education soon became apparent. He was dismissed for general irresponsibility and packed off to Canada as apprentice to a group of cotton-mill machine fitters. This new experience was taken up with enthusiasm. Fuller profited greatly from dealing with imported machinery, for the replacement of worn or defective parts not locally available provided an excellent exercise in technical ingenuity. His diligence was rewarded by his returning to Harvard—only to be dismissed again for lack of sustained interest. Though Fuller records his deep sense of shame at having again hurt his family by this second expulsion, he eagerly accepted the chance to get back into "the live economic pattern." From 3:00 P.M. till 5:00 A.M. he lugged beef, and studied market distribution, refrigeration, and accounting in various New York and New Jersey branches of Armour & Company, rising to the post of assistant cashier in two years.

World War I intervened, and after several attempts to enlist, Fuller was accepted for the Navy in 1917. Shortly afterward he married Anne Hewlett, the eldest daughter of James Monroe Hewlett, a man whom Fuller acknowledges as an important source of inspiration. Through this marriage Fuller received his first introduction to practical building, and his thoughts on design at this time must have been influenced by both Anne (who had recently left design school) and her father, who was by then a distinguished architect, mural painter, and stage designer.[3] Fuller's years in the Navy, between 1917 and 1919, afforded him the kind of education which Harvard had failed to provide. His boyhood excitement with boatbuilding, sailing, and related techniques found pragmatic scope in wide naval experience, from small-craft commands to duties in large fleet operations. The atmosphere of precise mathematics and exquisite timing required by navigation, ballistics, and the logistics of mass tonnage movements engendered a regard for "anticipatory" procedures which pervades his later theory.

His first two inventions were gestated in this period. One, a seaplane rescue mast and boom, earned him a special course award to the United States Naval Academy in 1917, and the

other, the design conception of a "jet stilt" vertical take-off
aircraft, was later brought to model stage and partially incorporated in the Dymaxion car of 1927 (plate 21). During
the war, he also edited the naval monthly, *Convoy*, and afterward compiled the official statistics of the whole Atlantic
troop-carrying operation. After the armistice, Fuller assisted
in the first transoceanic radio tie-up, from the U.S.S. *George
Washington* in Brest harbor to Arlington, Virginia. In 1919
he returned to industry as assistant export manager with
Armour & Company; this was followed by a brief period as
national sales manager with the Kelly Springfield Truck
Company.

Fuller's life took an important turn in 1922 for, together
with his father-in-law, he founded the Stockade Building
System to manufacture and develop Hewlett's invention: a
new type of fibrous concrete building block. In the same year,
his first daughter died, having suffered in turn a series of
epidemic infections aggravated by poor housing conditions
due to the war. This profound personal tragedy clouded the
next five years and, although Fuller continued in building
with enormous energy (setting up four plants and supervising
one hundred and fifty building constructions), the poor conditions he encountered in the industry intensified his gloom.[4]
He refers to this period as ". . . five years' experience within the most ignorant and most prodigious of men's fumbling
activities: that sub-industry activity of men, in fortuitous
agglomeration of sheltering and dwelling facilities."

Fuller's interpretation of his daughter's death as a personal
augury of the failure of over-all "design" evidenced in socie-
tal breakdown conditions like war, was now compounded with
the chaos and lack of foresight he found in craft building. He
became preoccupied with the discrepancy between society's
ability to plan and utilize the full potential of an advanced
technology for war and emergency purposes and the fractional, haphazard application of this capacity to the requirements of ordinary living.

The growing pressure of these thoughts was brought to a
head in 1927 when, shortly after the birth of his second
daughter, the Stockade Company was suddenly taken out of
his hands through changes in financial control. These two
events, not unusual in themselves, precipitated a complete
change in Fuller's life direction. He accepted their conjoined

occurrence as a profound comment on all of his previous thought and action. Implicit in his welcome of a new life responsibility was the realization of his own "manifold ineptitudes" in relation to his wider responsibility. The loss of Stockade showed him that he had been naïve in assuming any identity of his direction and interests with commercial interests. In his own affairs he also discerned the same lack of awareness and foresight which he found disturbing in the building industry and other areas of society. The simultaneity and complexity of such critical moments in life are difficult to convey adequately. Since 1927 Fuller obviously has been possessed of certain deep, personal, and very powerful intuitions about man's place in, and relation to, his world. He emerged from this period of emotional crisis and acute self-analysis with an urgent and desperate resolve to fulfill what he has termed his "blind date with principle."

He determined henceforth to eschew all future notion of direct financial gain and conventional success, and to devote himself solely to exploring toward "an art and science of generalized and anticipatory design competence." This, to be applied immediately to areas of prior human need, like housing, would seek to obviate present chaos and misery by taking advantage of all relevant, scientifically evolved principles in comprehensively designed solutions to be fully implemented by the most advanced technological means available. It was also clear that such "design" thinking could no longer be locally restricted in theory and application but, with regard to current accelerating trends, had to be predicted in terms of world needs eventually extending to encompass all areas of man's environmental requirements.

The year 1927 is the central pivot of Fuller's life, and within its span are located many of the events and ideas which determine his later work.

Following rapidly on the crisis, which fixed his personal energies in their unitary direction, came Fuller's publication of the "4D" and "4D Timelock" essays.[5] This privately printed book sums up his massive intellectual stocktaking at this time, and outlines many of the basic propositions from which later formulations of his design philosophy derive.

From the outset, Fuller's thinking is comprehensive; each development proceeds from consideration of its largest and most universal context, then goes on to local and more immediate aspects which present themselves. Among the many drawings accompanying "Timelock" is a World Town Plan sketch (plate 1) showing a number of multi-deck houses located around the earth, forming part of a global, air-maintained-and-distributed shelter service. This assumption of world housing as the only operable context within which the local solution may be sought is typical of Fuller's strategy.

He underlines that such solutions must embrace universal requirements—they must satisfy and nurture the broad range of human functions in terms of over-all performance and production. The world housing problem was, and is, such that it cannot be solved by the obsolete craft building industry. The volume of production necessary to meet immediate emergency demand and to anticipate further needs could only be achieved through advanced scientific and industrial means. Therefore, Fuller sought the requisite technical advantage within shipbuilding and aircraft technology since these seemed to embody the most advanced deployment of such means then available. The automobile industry of this time was mass-producing a large and complex unit comparable to a "house" —five million cars in 1925 as against half a million single-family dwellings in the same year. The automobile industry, however, lacked the "maximum performance per pound of material invested" which Fuller invoked as one of his initial referents. The adoption of such criteria is a key to the radical nature of all Fuller's designing. He proceeds from the initiation and statement of a problem to a review of the means available for its solution, and to the analysis of these in re-

16 lation to over-all requirements—then, and only then, does he pass to actual design and reduction to practice.

Fuller's first house designs of 1927 clearly reflect these methods. Maximal solution is sought in the large multi-deck apartment houses, in which the hexagonal deck planes are suspended by tension cables—on the wire-wheel principle— from a central tower of high-pressure inflated duraluminum tubes, with all compressive and tensile loading balanced out in taut triangulation (plates 2–5). Frame rigidity is secured by bracing ground-anchored cables (plate 4). This central mastlike tower contains the mechanics for services like elevators, air conditioning, and waste disposal, energy outlets for cooking and laundry utilities, and bathroom units which may be separately manufactured and flexibly installed. Pneumatically surfaced floors are supported on a three-way grid tubular construction, with vacuum cleaning elements built in. The entire house is enclosed in double-pane glass of different opacities for varying functions, and indirect lighting is diffused from the central mast and is subject to adjustments in intensity and color.

Fuller calculated the weight of a standard twelve-deck version of this house at 45 tons—including swimming pool, gymnasium, library decks, accessories, and furniture—and calculated that, if mass-produced, it would cost approximately $23,000. It was designed to be air-delivered by a dirigible of 90-ton load capacity, and erected in one day on a base which enclosed septic and fuel tanks. The United States dirigible of that time was 700 feet long, and the house was 190 feet long in horizontal loading position. While designing different versions of this house, Fuller experimented with aerodynamic shielding (to reduce air drag and heat loss) as an economic method of structure and heating (plates 3 and 5). In certain versions, wind energy provided an auxiliary power source, through rotary generators, so that the whole complex was designed, like a ship, to function for long periods of time, free of public utilities, sewage disposal, water supply, and other services.

The minimal five- or six-room single-family dwelling, associated with the design of these multiple shelters, is the version more familiar, through its later name adopted in 1929, of Dymaxion House. This title compresses Fuller's repeated use of the words "dynamism," "maximum," and "ions." It is expressive of "maximum gain of advantage from minimal energy input," a term which he regarded as a technological principle: that the largest dividend of human advantage from the least investment of energy and materials may be achieved by the over-all employment of scientific and technical means. Several fully detailed scale models of this house were made and used by Fuller in his lectures. Structurally, it has the same wire-wheel tensional integrity of the multi-deck version, but with only two suspended decks (plates 6–8). The upper deck, with a partial roof canopy and parapet, is conceived as an open-air relaxation area. The deck below, enclosed in double-pane vacuum glazing, contains two bedrooms, two baths, living room, study, and "service" room. This deck roofs the garage and yard space on the ground level. Mechanical core elements in the mast provide lighting, plumbing, and air conditioning. The centralized lighting system is indirect, with intensity and color controls in each room, thus saving separate wiring and fixtures.

The laborsaving mechanics designed into this house were extremely sophisticated for the period, and many which were originally thought to be quite impractical have gradually come into circulation and been widely imitated over the years. Floor to ceiling units, flexible dividers of the internal space, housed utilities and simultaneously provided storage through a system of revolving shelves and hangers. Automatic laundry and dishwashing (which dried and returned the objects to storage) were incorporated into the system—plus an incinerator disposal unit. Folding concertina-type doors, photoelectric cell operated, were pneumatic and silent, as was the flooring. Compressed air and vacuum units took care of all cleaning and dusting. Balancing the detailed provision of light, sound, and space control in the physical environment, the "study" functioned as an intellectual "conning" or control room, with provision for anticipated radio/TV, maps, and globes, in addition to typewriter, mimeograph, and calculators housed in revolving bookshelves.

This house, designed as 40 feet in height and 50 feet in diameter, was broken down into component packages for air delivery and one day assembly on the site (plate 7). Total weight, including all built-in furniture and accessories, was to be 6,000 pounds. Production estimates varied from 25 to 40 cents per pound—but that was in terms of a mass produc-

18   tion schedule which would manufacture in just one day the total yearly output of the craft industry. The Dymaxion House was never intended as a design for a unique, one-of-a-kind building; its true function was to be the prototype for a world-wide housing industry, similar in scope to the auto, ship-building, or airplane industries but different in that it would rent its products on a service, repair, and new model replacement basis rather like a telephone company. Fuller's insistence on this aspect has been criticized as frivolous, but is validated today by the huge extension of such rental and credit facilities. He gave cost of initiating such an industry as around $100,000,000 (pointing out that the new Ford of the day cost $43,000,000 to develop its first single unit, but subsequent reproductions only cost $500 retail, or around 22 cents per pound).

This was not an architectural masterwork in any of the accepted senses of uniqueness or permanence but was, rather, a rigorously controlled experiment in environment control. Nor was it an aesthetic dream house carefully furnished and decorated to preserve a fixed continuity of experience but was, instead, a delicately adjustable and unobtrusive "servo-mechanism"—in which full creative control was invested in the occupant, with no design-imposed limitations. To the idea of a house as a cavelike shelter *against* the elements, Fuller opposed the concept of an "invisible energy valve," used as mediator between man and environment, which allowed him to "phase" the elements (or nature) into his required patterns of experience and use. Natural energy could be channeled directly into work as electricity or air conditioning, or it could be impounded in batteries for future use. This was not simply an aesthetic "machine to live in" but a machine like the auto or airplane, designed to extend the potential of living—either in or out! The 35-year-old Dymaxion House is of considerable importance because it incorporates many of Fuller's main principles.[6]

The Dymaxion House was far in advance of its time, compared to other architectural work around 1927.[7] In this year also, the Deutscher Werkbund exhibited the work of the vanguard of the modern movement in its Weissenhof housing scheme. Taking part in this were Mies van der Rohe, Le Corbusier, J. J. P. Oud, and others—an assembly which later gave rise to the designation "International Style." Though specifically related to rational fabrication methods for low-cost dwellings, the Weissenhof housing scheme was distinguished mainly by the aesthetic treatment of internal and external layouts, and the formally pleasing qualities of its façade, roof, and fenestration treatments. Concealed by the stucco, fabrication still lagged behind current technical possibility.

Fuller's general condemnation of the architecture and building industry of his time, in relation to mass housing needs, may have been fortified by his location in an area where social legislation and control had long tended to be minimal. In Europe, the drive toward providing solutions had been under way since the late 19th century, although many schemes literally did not get off the ground for lack of fully industrialized prototypes designed in real manufacturing terms. Fuller's criticism of the International Style as a "fashion inoculation," though harsh, is quite justified, for he sees that it was overconcerned with the *visual* aspect of both buildings and machine products, while structural function and capability had passed over into the *invisible* terms of hidden alloy strengths and instrumental tolerances. He suggests further that the International Style never invoked the real technological criteria which lie in over-all performance per weight of material invested.[8]

The history of the modern movement has been one of a long-standing flirtation with technology; but the marriage seems never to have been consummated. The emphasis of the discipline for some time has lain with the visual manipulation of the formal and symbolic elements of building. One feels that the *invisibility* of structural function has been intuitively recognized, but increasingly sidetracked aesthetically into the creation of spatial effects: the *ambiguity* of inside/outside in the glass wall, the *dematerialization* through use of glass at corners (as in the Gropius *Faguswerke*), the reflections in the great curtain walls (like the United Nations Building), the *feeling* of lightness given to massive concrete structures by mounting the whole on slender *pilotis*. This has given us a very great architecture whose individual works are superbly poetic evocations of certain aspects of machine technology. But such an emphasis may in fact operate negatively because we so manifestly require real technological solutions to minimal shelter needs.

20   Though Fuller based his house on current aircraft technology,[9] he foresaw a considerable time lag in the full availability, in quantity production, of the materials necessary for mass production. In the years that followed, until his next full-scale shelter projects in the early 1940's, he applied himself to a wide program of intensive personal research and to the practical development through industrial means of many technical innovations anticipated in his early projects. Throughout the early depression years, he lectured and demonstrated the Dymaxion House, and from this period dates his friendship with many artists, among whom were the novelist Christopher Morley and the sculptor Isamu Noguchi (in whose Greenwich Village studio the house model was exhibited), who later made a remarkable bust of Fuller in stainless steel.

The middle period of Fuller's work can be roughly grouped around areas of major achievement: the theme of industrialized housing; studies in structural principles and logistics; and world economic planning which Fuller undertook as necessary to eventual realization of his ideas on housing. These groups demonstrate clearly the coherent pattern of research and exploration by which the years 1928–46 are characterized.

Extended geographic and social mobility is one of the prime features of our era. Developments in airplanes, helicopters, and more recently "hovercraft," increasingly free man from dependence on his overland road and rail networks. If shelter is to be brought to parity with these advanced environment tools, and is to be capable of swift deployment to any desired location, it should share this developed autonomy. Fuller's view of truly mobile environment control is one which would free man from dependence, also, on local land supply lines of power, water, sanitation, so that the house would be able to function autonomously, either completely or for long periods. Stimulated by examples in ships and aircraft, Fuller incorporated a design for economical water usage in the Dymaxion House, creating a system of filtering, sterilization, and recirculation of water for different purposes after use. The toilets were envisioned as a sealed packaging system requiring no water, wastes being mechanically packaged and stored for collection by the chemical processing industry. The direction toward full autonomy obviously lay in reassessing bathroom and toilet facilities and in the overall use of economical sharing and conversion energy systems employing mechanical core principles and utilizing, wherever possible, the naturally impinging energies of wind, sun, and rain as part of the total energy accounting.

Research undertaken for the Pierce Foundation of the American Radiator Company, in 1931, enabled Fuller to develop the first fully equipped bathroom and toilet unit (plates 9–11) as an integral mass-production item, as well as detailed schemes for a mass produceable utilities-core linking kitchen, heating, and lighting. The bathroom unit was reworked (with the Phelps-Dodge Corporation in 1936), in a version which included ventilating, lighting, and heating elements as well as complete plumbing. It was formed of four die-pressed sections which were bolted together for assembly and then required only connection. Though not strictly autonomous, it allowed easy conversion to an autonomous system. The combined unit, including all necessary bathroom facilities, was successfully developed to the prototype stage, and twelve models were eventually installed in various test places. It was not mass produced because the manufacturers felt that it might meet with resistance from plumbing interests, due to the fact that it could be taken out, like a refrigerator, when people moved, and just plugged into the next house.

The Mechanical Wing design of 1940 took these projects a stage further, by combining all mechanical and energy requirements into one package mounted on an "A frame" auto trailer (plate 12). Grouped around a small diesel engine (as energy unit with air compressor and electrical generator) was one of the unit bathrooms with a sealed packaging and chemical disposal apparatus, and a kitchen/laundry unit complete with sink, cooking range, and refrigerator. Also included in the bathroom was a "fog gun" device using a high pressure spray mixture of water and detergent which cleaned and massaged simultaneously, the whole operating on only one pint of water. This latter conception of the mechanics of personal cleansing demonstrates the rigor of Fuller's method and his willingness to explore any strategy which might forward eventual design performance. His continued assertion in this area is that "the design evolution must go beyond the surface. It must employ as scientific an approach to cleansing and heating the human being as is employed in the design of present electronic communications apparatus."[10]

The Autonomous Living Package of 1949 (plates 18–20) further elaborated the earlier Mechanical Wing project. Fuller directed a student group to take what he called a "Trial Balance Inventory . . . a comprehensive picture of the standards of living as advanced to A.D. 1949." The setting of this problem was an imagined evacuation of a city, in which each family of six persons would be allowed one trailer unit, 8' x 8' x 25'. This unit should contain all living facilities necessary—and with no lowering of standards. Teams went through stores and manufacturers' inventories in the area checking lists compiled against Fuller's Universal Requirements schedule. These were correlated and the final package assessed. It ranged through washing machines, refrigerators, stoves, gardening, wood and metalwork tools, complete furnishings, books, radios, cameras, projectors, darkroom equipment—everything down to musical instruments! This whole luxury package was calculated to cost around $18,000 and to weigh 9,000 pounds (minus original packing materials). Economic reappraisal reduced these figures to a standard assembly cost of $6,000 which under mass production, for sale like an "automobile package," could have been reduced to sell for approximately $2,000. At this stage, such a unit was designed to fit into a 50-foot-diameter geodesic dome, giving complete furnishing and mechanics for fully autonomous operation.

From his studies of mechanical and heating requirements for housing, Fuller suggests that "energy and gases involve unique local patternings which may be utilized to provide cooling and heating energy by means of preferred shell shapes and vent control, requiring only relatively small amounts of introduced mechanical energy." From this comes the wrap-around windshield of the 1927 multi-deck dwellings (plates 3 and 5), which is further refined in the Wichita House (plate 27) whose circular shape fulfills a similar function. In the later geodesic structures, the naturally streamlined form is even more efficiently employed, and closer atmospheric control may be gained by raising and lowering the whole external shell. In dealing with the internal effect of outer form, Fuller points out that "division into cubic rooms linked by low doorways which trap convected air in ceiling pools maintains an over-all thermal capacity of less than five per cent, the dweller being served usually by a random drifting from super-hot pockets surrounding radiators." The heat loss of forms being directly proportional to their wind resistance, that of a cubical house is approximately four times that of a hemispherical house of equal volume (plate 3). Fuller's "energy valving principle" in housing leads him then to state that interior and exterior aerodynamics are a fundamental of the essentially visible design problem of environment controls.

The Dymaxion Deployment Unit of 1940–41 and the Twin Dymaxion Deployment Unit were practical statements—even proof—of the foregoing ideas, and were the first of Fuller's

24 projects to attain mass production (plates 13–17). Produced in association with the Butler Manufacturing Company, this design was a conversion of their corrugated grain storage bin to a dwelling unit. The change was effected mainly by replacing the standard top with a compound curvature roof and by adding skylights, ventilator, porthole windows, and a door (plate 13); walls and ceiling were lined with Fiberglas-backed wallboard (plate 17). Designed for wartime use as radar stations, dormitories, hospitals, etc., each 20-foot-diameter unit, fully furnished, cost $1,250 as a complete package with kerosene icebox and stove. Production reached 1,000 units per day, but this figure was curtailed by reallocation of steel priorities. A considerable number of these units were used in locations with widely differing climates. In accordance with the ideas outlined above they were completely satisfactory— even in such extreme heat conditions as those of the Persian Gulf.

Dymaxion transport—the swift deployment of autonomous dwelling facilities to any desired region—presumes a similar flexibility in the local transport of occupants, as well as of their social and supply needs. In planning the first Dymaxion House complex, Fuller included such a transport auxiliary, in model form—an "auto-airplane," capable of highway or aerial travel. This was evolved from the "hoverable" jet-stilt aircraft, powered with separate angularly orientable turbine jets for full maneuverability, which he had paper-designed during his World War I naval aviation service (plate 21).

In 1933, he returned to this problem. Fuller views the Dymaxion Transport, built then, as an evolutionary phase of the more complex air/land vehicle—a design stage which separated the cross-wind taxiing from other land contact performance problems (plates 22 and 23). Aeronautically streamlined and three wheeled (with two-front-wheel drive and single rear-wheel steering), this eleven-passenger car was capable of speeds of over one hundred miles per hour using a standard V8 90 hp rear-mounted engine. It was extremely maneuverable, traveling over plowed fields and other rough terrain with ease. Radically designed (far more so, for example, than the Burney "streamliner" of 1930), it also predated the first mass-produced Airflow, the 1934 Chrysler, and featured many more automotive innovations. Now, after almost thirty years, it would look quite at home on the road, a kind of crossbred cousin of the present Isetta and Heinkel "bubblecars" and the Volkswagen bus. A later version, developed for Kaiser in 1945, and subsequently improved (plate 24), was a design which used three 15–25 hp engines mounted as detachable units with wheel and drive. After the vehicle started, only one engine needed to be used, giving a running average of 40–50 miles per gallon.

Fuller had early suggested a time lag of some twenty-five years before the material resources would be available for full implementation of the Dymaxion House program. In late 1944, while serving with the U.S. Foreign Economic Administration, he prepared a scheme for the postwar conversion of the aircraft industry to housing purposes. A developing labor shortage, due to lack of worker accommodations, was seriously holding up production at one of the major centers, with the result that Fuller was invited to explore the possibilities of his scheme. The resultant house prototype, the Wichita House of 1945–46, produced in the Beech Aircraft plant at Wichita, Kansas, logically sums up his researches of this middle period. It was engineered, using aircraft tools in assembly-line techniques, as a full-scale pilot model for a production run.

Circular in form, the Wichita House was a structure of aluminum, steel, and plexiglass, tensionally suspended from a central mast by cables, and braced to the ground (plates 25–29). Similar in structure to the 1927 Dymaxion House, in employing the double wire-wheel principle, the Wichita House, because of advances in alloy chemistry and metallurgy, presented a more economically refined structure with vastly increased strength for less material investment. The 22-foot mast, formed of only seven 3-inch stainless-steel tubes, weighed 72 pounds and was capable of carrying the entire house plus the weight of over one hundred and twenty people. The steep pitch of the 1927 house now gave way to a low-slung compound curvature roof, within which were located the compression/tension system of the double wire-wheel complex and all supporting tension members.

The living space was divided into two bedrooms with bathrooms, living room, kitchen, and entry hall on the main living deck, with garage space below (plate 26). (Two-deck models were also planned.) The living room, with two balconies and all-round double-pane plexiglass windows, was diamond shaped, measuring 28 feet on the long axis (plate

28). Doors were of the folding screen type, and all storage elements were located in the dividing partitions. Lighting was indirect throughout. Household mechanics were all centralized around the mast, with their "energy accounting" such that all air conditioning, heating, refrigeration, laundry, and dish-washing units linked together to operate at the previous cost of a single coal-burning furnace. The housetop ventilator gave ten complete changes of air per hour, which could be passed through the conditioner for temperature control. House maintenance was reduced to a minimum, all structural surfaces being of nonoxidizing materials.

In limited mass production the complete house was calculated to retail at $6,500. Full volume-production of 500,000 per year would have reduced this further to $3,700. In aircraft terms, this was a relatively simple product, having only about 200 parts, as opposed to the 2,500 in current plane production schedules. Houses were designed to come off the assembly line crated and transportable (for $100 more) to any part of the country (plate 29). Visitors to the completed furnished prototype were unanimous in their approval of its spaciousness and the luxury of its appointments; in all, 3,700 purchase applications were registered. But this realization of Fuller's industrialized dwelling was not to be. The war came to an end and capital was directed elsewhere in the industry, so that the whole venture was abandoned for lack of funds to support the necessary initial steps. As a result of this, Fuller resolved never again to allow any of his projects to be so wholly at the mercy of any such speculative capital interests.

It is interesting to observe, at the close of this period, the strange polarity of inner and outer events which produces a characteristic pattern in Fuller's life and is reflected in his thought. His early experience of deeply felt personal tragedy, crossed with the loss of the Stockade Company, triggered off the Dymaxion exploration. Similarly, the development of the Wichita project paralleled the breakthrough into Geodesic/ Tensegrity principles. Its failure freed Fuller's energies again and was immediately followed by the upsurge of geodesic domes and their outward global explosion ten years later.

The "house" development is marked by the transition from *inner* mechanical to *outward* shell aspects. His own expressed emphasis is on the internal "invisible" energy structure as determining the externally visible form. But "inner" and "outer" may obviously be regarded as simply labels describing the complementary interactive aspects of the whole. We shall again meet this view of an "events" polarity in oscillating inner and outer concentric patterns when we consider Fuller's geometry and the general propositions of his design philosophy.

The Wichita House brings full circle this roughly twenty years' exploratory period. Before going on to consider the geodesic/tensegrity structures which developed out of this phase, we should note the researches in the charting and planning of world industrialization which ran, concurrently with Fuller's housing programs, through this middle period.

Though Fuller has considerable verbal capacities, much of his communication has been concerned with the visual nonverbal means by which complex relations and behaviors may be grasped in a more simultaneous fashion. During his work with Phelps Dodge, as technical consultant to *Fortune* magazine, and with the U.S. Foreign Economic Administration, he developed novel modes of charting which graphically showed the complex historical relations of man's material progress through advances in science and technology, and the political and economic effects or consequences. These were not simply visualized statistics, but were, rather, more operable, visual tools making possible the rapid scanning of trends, allowing the prediction of emergent patterns against which research and production might be gauged (plate 30). To Phelps Dodge, for example, such work had much immediate practical value, as in correlating the global "scrapping and re-use" cycles of the various metals with which they were concerned. As Fuller suggests in his book, *Nine Chains to the Moon*, published at that time, industries might relate their schedules to such cycles and *rent* their materials for production against eventual scrapping and return to the stockpile, e.g., copper in autos would have a use period of approximately eight years, while in ships this would be about twenty years. Processing material for *Fortune* surveys on United States and world industrialization, Fuller worked out a number of new formulations—such as the replacement of industrial value terms like Tonnage and Man-hours, by Energy[11]—which was

28 more expressive of the over-all industrial content invested in products.

Also published during this period was Fuller's minimal distortion *Air Ocean World Map,* a new cartographic projection which shows the world's land masses as one main island-grouping in the "one-world" ocean (plate 32). By its employment of a triangulated great-circle grid, it allows more accurate plotting of great-circle air routes on a plane surface and facilitates the more comprehensive view of geographical relations of resource location, trade routes, etc. Associated with this is the World Energy Map showing population and available industrial energy distribution in whole terms (plate 31).

The latest development in this family of world "social navigation" aids, which had been gestating for some years, is called the Geoscope Dynamic Display. In its present form, this is planned basically as a miniature earth sphere 200 feet in diameter, correctly oriented in location, with geographical and other data placed accurately on its surface (plate 33). Wired with 10 million surface points, electronically controlled by a computer, this will furnish a giant spherical television screen—allowing for the accurate display of dynamic world patterns at variably controlled display speeds. Viewing the stars through the semitransparent land masses, from the center of the "earth," will locate man in the universe, and the electronic display facilities will enable him to see and comprehend patterns far beyond his normal perceptive power. World historical patterns of change may be observed at normal, accelerated, or slow-motion speeds; but variables may be introduced to assess factors governing change. One could view in a few minutes a flow of men, processes, and materials that actually took many years to occur. The Geoscope, by bringing such comprehensive patterning within normal mental reach, can obviously assist greatly in education and the solution of many complex problems.

Other projects of a similar nature, providing advantages for general as well as "design" education, are now under way in the Design Research and Development branch of the Design Department of Southern Illinois University, where Fuller has been Research Professor since 1959.

While the Wichita House sums up many of Fuller's ideas on the internal mechanical aspects of housing, the geodesic domes which follow are the culmination of his parallel researches into structural geometry. Fuller's early preoccupation with geometry stems partially from his experience in navigation and ballistics. Here geometry is a working tool with which one measures and anticipates natural energetic forces—calculating forward "energy" events in time, relative to complex, interactive factors. In the swift and accurate computation which this entails, Fuller probably gained insight into the requirements of a more rational co-ordinate geometry.

The evolution of his Energetic and Synergetic Geometry, from which geodesic/tensegrity structuring is derived, arose out of Fuller's main explorations toward maximal advantage in environment control structures through effective energy accounting. Fuller uses the term "energetic" to refer to separated and individual working parts of a system: its "local" aspects. "Synergy" is used to define the way in which whole systems act as more than the simple sum of their parts, thus containing features which cannot be predicted from the behavior of separate parts or local events.

Energy, as manifested in structural systems, is polarized into "push" and "pull" energy, compression and tension. Fuller observed that, historically, man's structures had been largely dominated by the greater compressive strengths available, mainly stone piled up in great mass. Earlier tensile strengths, such as those found in natural fiber cordages, were restricted in use by material variation and impermanence, and hence were employed only as local and secondary stiffening, as in ships' rigging and bracing guy ropes. Compression has inherent limitations of length relative to thickness, so that a compressed member tends to fail when flexed under stress. In tension, however, strengths seem to be relatively unlimited. Loads tend to increase over-all length, contracting the diameter so that the member becomes more cohesive under stress which, being distributed throughout all dimensions, allows loads to be applied at any point. Dramatically rapid advances in metallurgy and alloy chemistry now give man tensional capacities far in excess of those available in compression.

In his 1927 structures, by separating compression and tension energies into their most advantageous form in relatively short compressive members combined with long cable and rod tensions, Fuller intuitively arrived at his structural principle of discontinuous compression/continuous tension, thus employing each at its maximum operational strength. His most typical use of differing forms of this tensional integrity, or "tensegrity," has been developed through the triangulated spherical networks of the geodesic domes. An extended review of the principles of energetic and synergetic geometry upon which they are based is beyond our present purpose, but some brief notation of its development may be useful (plates 34–39).

Starting with "universe" as the prime energy system, Fuller sought the minimal arrangement of vectors, or force lines, which would mirror the complexity of the whole system, and yet be comprehensible and maneuverable. Through the closest packing of spheres around a central nucleus, he arrived at a fourteen-faced geometrical form (plates 34, 35).[12] The linear extract of this polyhedron, all of whose sides are equal in length to each other and to the distance of any vertex to the center, Fuller calls a Vector Equilibrium. This forms an isotropic vector matrix—a system in which all vectors are the same length and all vertexes equidistant from one another. It is an omnidirectional concentric topological form which furnishes a dynamic coordinate system, accommodating the requirements of many complex physical laws, and providing analogues of their functions.

This complex whole form, compound of octahedron and tetrahedron (often called the "octet truss"), phases down into component tetrahedrons. The tetrahedron, therefore, a four-sided triangular-faced figure (plate 36), seems to be the minimal dimensional energy system, or vector configuration. All other figures may be subdivided into tetrahedrons but no tetrahedron divides into a polyhedron with less than four sides; thus the tetrahedron probably represents the basic energy configuration of universal structure.[13]

Among the complex laws which may be demonstrated with the use of Vector Equilibrium is that of "precession," which refers to the effect of one system in motion upon another: always at resulting angles of deflection other than the straight line of 180 degrees. In an all-motion universe, all phenome-

non interactions are precessional; lines of force are not 31
straight but tend to curvilinear paths. These paths are inherently "geodesic," i.e., the shortest distance between points
on a curved or spherical surface. With the automatic tendency
of energy in networks to triangulate, Fuller assumed that
the most economical structural energy web might be derived
through the fusion of tetrahedron and sphere (see plate 37).
(The sphere encloses most space with least surface and is
strongest against internal pressure, the tetrahedron encloses
least space with most surface and is strongest against external
pressure.) This may be accomplished via the icosahedron, a
multiphase tetra, all of whose vertexes lie on the surface of
a sphere. By exploding this form onto the sphere and sym-
metrically subdividing its faces, we arrive at the three-way
great-circle grid of the geodesic structure.[14]

Enclosing the most volume with maximum resistance to
external and internal stresses, this structure sheds loading on
any part through its entire network of compression and tension integrity: destruction or removal of whole segments does
not impair this phenomenon. In simpler geodesic structures
the same structural member may, in use, alternate between
being stretched and compressed. In more refined tensegrity
structuring, compression members are separate from tension
members, with the former reduced to short rods or struts not
in contact with one another but integrated with the continu-
ously joined tension members.

It is important to note that there are no inherent size
limitations. As the system gets larger, the number, or frequency, of triangulation is increased. Furthermore, its relative
strength grows at a faster rate than the weight of structure
required; as more members are used the ratio of slenderness
to weight is relatively decreased. The structure grows relatively lighter as it enlarges, like a balloon membrane. Hence,
at very great dimensions such structures would tend to zero
dimensions, to comparative invisibility. Employing materials
in a way that is congruent with their subvisible cohesive
principles, this system admits to structural use many materials
and techniques not usually applied in building.[15]

The first phase development of geodesic structures underlines Fuller's resolution, at the end of the Wichita project, to
avoid the initial exploiting of his design realizations through
commercial means. The growing number of invitations from

universities and other schools enabled him to develop the geodesic dome to its fully practical form in a series of student projects. These seminar programs were unique in that functional research and complete industrial prototyping of structures was carried out, in schemes lasting on an average of from one to six weeks, with student groups of varying years and attainment. Work was thus produced which was far in advance of any in industry, and in a fraction of the time which such external agencies would have required for this complex development. The structural capacity of the Octet (Vector Equilibrium) Truss was also investigated by Fuller during this period (plates 40–41, 43, 47, 83). Functioning on similar three-way grid load-shed principles, this may be utilized for great clear-span cantilevers as horizontal flooring or flat platforms.

A great number and variety of experimental prototypes have been produced in these university programs (plates 42, 44–45, 49–51, 53–58). They remain a continuing feature of Fuller's design development, and he has now conducted similar projects in many parts of the world. The diversity of materials and techniques employed may be seen in the illustrated examples (plates 46–47, 52, 59).

The first large-scale industrial breakthrough in geodesic structuring occurred in 1953, when the Ford Company commissioned a dome to cover their Rotunda Building (plates 60–64). A conventional steel dome would have weighed 160 tons, much more than the building could support. The geodesic structure, 93 feet in diameter, weighed only $8\frac{1}{2}$ tons, and was made of aluminum trusses in Octet formation with a final plastic skin covering. The inherent design advantages of the geodesic domes were so clearly apparent in this first public demonstration that there was an immediate demand for their use in many fields.

The following year, 1954, Fuller was asked by the U.S. Marine Corps to advise on a mobile shelter for forward-area use. The current system of tents, semipermanent and permanent structures, plus many special-purpose shelters, had become progressively redundant, and now tended to cancel out gains in speed and mobility available through improved flight technology. Altogether some 47 types of shelter were in use, requiring 2,900 items for construction. Because many buildings were left in place when units moved on, costs were repetitive. Initial exploration through various university projects, directed by Fuller, provided a number of first-stage solutions, ranging from a 36-foot-diameter dome for aircraft hangars down to a 14-foot-diameter paper-board shelter for six men. The latter, being expendable, was immediately nick-named the "Kleenex" house; it was one-third the weight of a tent, cost one-fifteenth as much, used less than ten dollars' worth of material, and packed into a smaller box!

The Marine Corps rigorously tested these and other proto-types for over two years (plates 65–67). Some were air-lifted by helicopter up to sixty miles across country, others given daylong 120 mph simulated wind-slam loads. They were deliberately rough-handled in daily test assemblies by untrained crews who still averaged only 135 minutes to put up a dome. Finally, one 42-foot-diameter dome which could be assembled in two different forms was reported as satisfy-ing 89 per cent of the shelter needs, and geodesics were adopted as general replacements for previous structures. The final report on this Marine Corps study described the new shelters as "the first basic improvement in mobile military shelters in the past 2,600 years," and stated that they re-quired only 3 per cent of the weight of former solutions, 6 per cent of the packaged volume, 14 per cent of the cost and less than 1 per cent of erection manhours. The total cost sav-ings would in the end amount to $45,000,000.

For Fuller, the practical success of this project was a vindi-cation of his initial premise, embodied in the Dymaxion House of 1927, of an environment-control facility air de-liverable to any part of the earth and fully designed to meet every requirement through the most efficient use of all in-vested energy. The early assumption of this premise now gave him a forward design advantage in forecasting such eventual emergent needs.

The Radomes of 1956 were a further trial of these prin-ciples. Structures were required, strong enough to function at sub-zero temperatures, in 150 mph winds, capable of air delivery and assembly in the brief working periods between climatic extremes operating in the Arctic DEW line area. In addition, they had to be permeable to radar beams. Fuller's solution to these problems was the 55-foot-diameter polyester Fiberglas domes (plates 71, 72) which were flown to the site and erected in 14 hours; they have withstood wind forces of

200 mph. These, and later models, are now in use in large numbers.

Similar requirements of delivery speed and special siting inaugurated the present use of geodesics on a world-wide scale in the United States Information Service's exhibition programs. The first 100-foot-diameter pavilion was designed and fabricated in six weeks for use at a trade fair in Kabul, Afghanistan (plate 74). This was delivered by one DC 4 aircraft, and erected by local labor in 48 hours. In 1959, a 200-foot-diameter dome was a major attraction of the United States Exhibit in Moscow (plate 82). Both the Radome and the Kabul geodesics were originated by Fuller's associated offices, Geodesics, Inc. and Synergetics, Inc., which now operate as self-supporting organizations, and have been associated with the engineering, development, and prototyping of many of the later structures. Since these early projects, almost 2,000 geodesic domes have been produced and are to be found in some forty countries of the world. More than 100 industrial licensees are now engaged in their manufacture, ranging from small units of an average 20-40-foot diameter in wood (plates 73, 75, 76), metal (plates 79, 84, 94), plastics (plate 87), paper-board, and other materials (plate 91), to the largest clear-span enclosures in existence, the present 380-foot-diameter Union domes.

Notwithstanding this large-scale application of Fuller's principles, his personal allegiance remains committed to his early goal of low-cost, high-grade family dwellings embodying the highest living standards for all people. More than one third of the world's population suffers from lack of even minimally adequate housing. Floods, storms, and other catastrophes render thousands homeless every year, and a growing population constantly adds to the urgency of an inadequately housed world population. In exploring emergency solutions, Fuller has particularly investigated the use of paper-board structures. Related to the Marine Corps "Kleenex" house, a 42-foot-diameter paper-board dome won the Milan Triennale Gran Premio in 1954 (plates 68–70). Full development of this project was held up until paper of sufficient wet-strength compression recently became available. The Monsanto Company's 22-foot-diameter Geospace dome, of Kraft paper and Styrofoam sandwich panel construction, reached mass production in 1961, and later that year 100

units were in use in Puerto Rico as emergency housing (plate
92). The importance of this type of structure lies in the enormous productive capacity already available in paper processing and printing plants around the world. Potential capacity of a large mill is around a million dome units a year—a production which would go some way toward meeting immediate needs. Another useful production feature is that assembly instructions, color coding, and any other required matter may be printed on the units as part of the process. Plastic coated, such domes have a long service life and excellent insulation qualities for either arctic or tropical conditions. In combination with domestic energy package developments in small "mechanical core" units, solar batteries, etc., these paper houses could be a powerful evolutionary tool in the raising of living standards in many depressed areas around the world.

Since his recent extensive travels in the Orient, Fuller has also worked on other solutions more immediately available through restricted local means. From initial field work on a bamboo, geodesic-tensegrity dome he has evolved a new system of "Basketry" tensegrity which promises as spectacular a structural gain over other geodesics as these have given over conventional structuring so far (plates 93, 98, 99–100). Development of this system was undertaken as a senior class project, in 1961, at Southern Illinois University. The resultant 72-foot-diameter, two-thirds spherical dome, 50 feet high at the center, encloses 4,000 square feet of floor area, and is the first full practical use of tensegrity as an environment enclosure, though many experimental fully spherical and mast type structures have been made. The framing of this dome, in 2″ x 4″ wood, is calculated at 25 cents per square foot enclosed, for the prototype, compared with $3 to $4 per square foot of orthodox framing. This dramatic material economy is afforded by the "discontinuous compression/continuous tension" principle, which, in this structure, allows wooden members to be bolted directly to one another without any extra hub-joining system. This new class of dome therefore opens up possibilities of phenomenally low fabrication costs, and may be produced using relatively simple technical facilities (as in the lumber industry), more readily available in areas where the need may be greatest.

The transition, from such relatively small structures for

36 single-family dwellings (see Fuller's home plates 88–90) to the very large domes already in use for industrial and other centralized purposes (plates 77, 78), underlines the flexibility of Fuller's constructional principles, and hints at the capacity of actual city-size enclosures functioning as environment space. Calculations for structures of one-hundred-acre span and even of two miles in diameter have been made (plate 103). At such great dimensions the structural members would be quite invisible, and their frequency such that the enclosure would be a gossamer-like membrane (plates 101, 102). The gain in control of physical environment factors would be tremendous. The recent Union and St. Louis Climatron structures are pilot examples of such emergent possibility.

The Union Tank Car Company's domes at Baton Rouge, Louisiana, and Wood River, Illinois, built in 1958 and 1961, are at present the largest clear spans in existence (plates 80, 81, 95). With a diameter of 384 feet and the height of a ten-story block at center, they cover 2½ acres for roughly 2 ounces of structural weight per cubic foot enclosed. Their one-eighth inch steel skin is thus relatively less than eggshell thin. The St. Louis Climatron, of 1960, 175 feet in diameter, and 70 feet high, forms part of a completely controlled environment system devised by Dr. F. W. Went which enables botanists to simulate many different climactic conditions in the same enclosure, without partitioning (plates 85, 86). Temperatures and humidity are automatically maintained and adjusted by a central computer.

In studies for domes to be built in Japan, one of which would be 750 feet in diameter, Fuller has investigated yet another tensegrity dome called "Aspension-tensegrity" (plates 96–97; see also plate 48). Designed to be factory woven, like a great fish net, this structure would rise "synergetically" on site from its folded form, by the outward pulling of a base ring on its edges. Viewed as an "adjustable" control system, similar to the Climatron, this dome would handle *external* variables through electronic and mechanical means. For example, although the dome is equal to earthquake or typhoon stress, heavy snow loads would require a structure of seventy times more weight—but such snows are infrequent in the Orient. Therefore, rather than use more structure, Fuller has incorporated infrared radiation so that the snow will be melted. Other low-frequency variables could be handled in a similar way.

In the swift evolution of these new types of structuring, one may more clearly discern the direction which has been implied in Fuller's researches since 1927. The minimal concept of "house" or "dwelling" as a fortress-like defense against inclement natural forces has been entirely revised. The task of the designer, architect, or engineer is now set within the larger context of devising delicately adjustable environment systems, controlling and utilizing natural forces, with a standard of performance on a par with man's other more highly developed environmental tools. In his endeavor to "do more with less," and to "phase" structural energy according to natural strategies, Fuller has arrived at forms which are analogous to those evolved in current studies of biological and cybernetic mechanisms—forms whose behavior approaches the dynamic equilibrium of self-adjusting systems. The viability of his structural forms in other hands, and in such "material" diversity, is also suggestive of their congruence with the principles governing natural structuring.

This reorientation is not directed toward the provision of more elaborate household gadgetry, nor is it simply toward a more pleasing external wrapping. Fuller seeks rather to free man's energies from absorption with the material means by which he gains, in so many cases, only a minimal survival advantage over environment. He suggests that this may be accomplished by the highest performance of scientifically designed "advantage" available now in our developed technological inventory. But this goal may only be sought today in terms of the whole human family—for just as contemporary industry now depends on the resources of the entire earth to function adequately, so, with the shrinking of the physical world, the continued well-being and prosperity of any one man, or nation of men, ultimately depends on that of all men.

Comprehensive Design Philosophy

The design philosophy of Buckminster Fuller is as many-faceted as the great structures which are part of its tangible realization. Like those structures, it has an integrity of principle which makes an operable whole, although the summary which follows is condensed to include only those aspects applicable to the structural directions previously described.

Fuller, seeking in 1927 for a working definition of "universe" or "nature," formulated such a definition as "the aggregate of all men's consciously apprehended and communicated experience." As operational premise, this assumes that man is an integral part of the universe and that all his environmental transactions, whether building, sleeping, plowing a field, or designing structures, form part of the total energy system. As defined out of his experience, this system is finite, so that energy, neither lost nor gained in nature, undergoes cycles of regenerative transformation. Each "energy" process or event is in dynamic progressive relation to all other processes and events; and the fundamental pattern of these interactive relations extends through the immediately visible, or median, level of ordinary everyday life outwardly to the macroscopic level of the galaxies and inwardly to the micro- and submicroscopic levels of molecular events.

Within this comprehensive assumption, art, science, and technology are merely local modes of organizing our experience of the universe. But, as Fuller says, "Nature confronts us as a going concern—she has no discernible separate departments in which she functions differently the one from the other." Undue emphasis on locally unique aspects may obscure the larger patterns operating in the universe—similar to the way in which energy events interact at different rates and magnitudes and at varying degrees of angular deflection, so "refracting" their fundamental causal relations. Study, or interpretation, therefore, where local, requires always to be related to the workings of the whole system. Where Fuller uses "energy" to refer to "the isolated differentiated behavior of nature," "synergy" describes "the unique behavior of whole systems as unpredicted by behavior of their parts, or respective subsystems' events." Whole studies are therefore both energetic and synergetic in their regard for the complex co-operative patterning that exists, a priori, in nature. From this viewpoint, in "designing" we locally rearrange the natural energy patterns to our immediate and future advantage. For maximal advantage, design then should be comprehensively oriented to employ such preferred patterns as we have been able to elicit from universal behavior, i.e., scientific laws.

Fuller sees the prime "design," or structural, event of our time as the completion of the table of atomic elements, giving a full basic inventory whose true functioning is invisibly located at the sub-molecular level. From this follows his assertion that, in reality "men do not build houses with materials. They merely organize visible-module structures comprised of subvisible module structures." With design as the visible ordering of subvisible energy events, there is no value division between natural and synthetic materials—synthesizing is a local rearranging of the basic element inventory.

Relation to the traditional canons of aesthetic judgment becomes tenuous. Formulas such as "truth to materials" and "form follows function" are inadequate because they are localized responses to the wholly visible aspects of natural processes continuous into their invisible, yet coherent macro- and micro-extremities. With new alloy and chemical strengths, function relative to material and form is truly not susceptible to vision. Materials and mechanical means should be evaluated in terms with no preconceived formal preference. No single design or structure within this scheme may be regarded as a traditional "masterwork" in the sense of a permanent artifact whose style may be emulated. Rather, a masterwork resides in the discovery of pure principle which may be freely employed and developed by others in many different forms. Permanence is obviously relative, and there is no implied end "solution"—only the continued flexible response to man's requirements which are in themselves a dynamic interplay of energy relationships in varying degrees of transformative change. The requirements of man, within this orientation, are considered in the widest sense, as extending beyond physically measurable well-being to the satisfaction of over-all psychophysical needs. The trend is not simply to increase the material paraphernalia of living, but rather progressively to dematerialize such means.

In reviewing man's historical progress, Fuller suggests that he has survived only by "anticipatory strategy," by his ca-

40 pacity consciously to organize his past experience against future contingency. The prime mode of ordering experience, what we now call Science, is the best form of such organization. Through this, man stores experience in technology which gives him advantage over material environment by replacing muscle power with principle externalized in the form of tools. Invisible principle, or "right," prevails over material "might."

Technical progress forms part of the general evolutionary pattern. From early craft tools created out of limited local experience and materials and operable by one man or few men, such as the dugout, canoe, or wheeled cart, we arrive at the fully industrialized environment tool—the ocean liner, the auto, and the airplane. At this phase, industry has become a complex co-operative phenomenon, embodying the universal experience of all men, and requiring global access to its necessary raw materials. Its nature implies mass production, and it tends, therefore, toward universal distribution for universal use. Fuller defines industrialization as "the objective, exact synergetic re-integration—into a comprehensive, common, regenerative advantage of man—of all the subjective, exact differentiated energy behaviors discovered by all the individual explorations of all history's exact scientists." Viewing the industrial complex as "mathematical principle in universe," he points to our industrial wealth resource as inexhaustible, lying as it does in the accumulated experience of all men through science. There can be no real depletion of this wealth because full-inventoried materials, or energy elements, are progressively recycled and re-used in regenerative fashion. "Science has hooked up the everyday plumbing to the cosmic reservoir." Man's evolution, therefore, may be predicated not wholly on natural selection or biological mutation, but also on full access to his accumulated universal experience, as more consciously modifying his forward progress.

Fuller's realization of the measures necessary to bring shelter to industrial parity with other developed advantages led directly to the inauguration of his particular design exploration. But he does not regard the application of full industrial potential to this, and other world problems, as implicit in the present phase of arbitrary commercial exploitation of resources. This end may only be accomplished by the emergence of a new social initiative: an initiative of design rather than political bias. Creative individuals, in our time, have largely relinquished such initiative to other agencies. Fuller suggests that the developed and proved competence of world architects and engineers in the handling of large-scale environment operations now requires that they resume this wider anticipatory planning function. He views such a comprehensive designer as a synthesis of artist, inventor, mechanic, objective economist, and evolutionary strategist, bearing the same relation to society in the new interactive continuities of world-wide industrialization that the architect bore to the respective dependencies of feudal society.

By setting the role of the architect and engineer within a larger context of broad responsibility, and by charging him with designing the means whereby full environment advantage may be shared by all men, Fuller emphasizes the inclusive nature of his philosophy. He implies that the responsibility for invention, or discovery, extends to encompass its safeguarding, or holding in trust, for the commonweal. Thus, he tempers the traditional idealism of the "pure" scientist or artist by his prior acceptance of the experience that men may act negatively as well as positively in the human situation. We have witnessed, in our own time, how the most integrative theories may, without such safeguarding, be turned into the most disintegrative fact.

In defining comprehensive design as a co-ordinate function capable of integrating other specialist studies, Fuller often quotes A. N. Whitehead: "In foreseeing an ultimate crisis in our society wherein the people who were responsible for putting things together would have fallen so relatively far behind the specialists in knowledge extension as to be practically incapable of comprehending the integral significance of the specialized findings. The integrators would be unable to co-ordinate and realize the commonwealth potentials opened up by the differentiators."[16] The way out of this dilemma, Fuller suggests, is an educational approach which would embrace at the outset the most advanced and comprehensive review of fundamental principles. Then, as these are mastered, the student is led progressively through their subdivision and application to more local and separate cases. This procedure, which Fuller has employed with spectacular results, is derived from his own design approach, for as we have noted, whether confronting "design," "dwelling," or

42 "nature," he always proceeds from the whole to the particular. This implies an *inversion* of conventional education—which proceeds from the elementary local aspect to the complex whole and is therefore more difficult as it advances. Fuller has always been preoccupied with the ways in which the most complex patterning and behaviors of the universe may be brought within mental reach and made part of man's everyday working experience.[17]

Through the more immediate results of Fuller's work, structures of great elegance affording dramatic functional performance may be viewed around the world. Its greater value, however, may lie in the wide influence of his philosophical approach. His coherent system of thought is a creative synthesis which embraces many significant areas of the social, industrial, scientific, and individual aspects of living. It represents a major attempt to outline a workable and comprehensible cosmology which endeavors to account for all physical and psychophysical phenomena behaviors within a field system of relations encompassing all known scientific laws and hypotheses. In assuming a finite universe, permeable to human thought (which though not simultaneously "knowable" may yet be comprehended through its rationally co-ordinate patterns), Fuller restores man to a comprehensive position in which he may exercise his full evolutionary initiative toward controlling his destiny. He avoids previous philosophical dilemmas of paired antitheses, like materialism versus idealism, by assuming an integral polarity in phenomena relations, in which apparently exclusive opposites are resolved into place as complementary interactive aspects of a whole process. Within this approach, Value is not ultimately material, but like thought may be externalized in a materially operable principle. Hence ethical assumptions gain new dignity as the embodiment of such Value principles, materially and durably evident in man's universal experience.

1. A New England journal associated with transcendentalism, a philosophical viewpoint shared by Emerson, Thoreau, and others, which has been described as "a cosmic idealism coupled with Yankee practicality, Puritan pugnacity, and grasp of fact." Thoreau's *Walden* is an experiment in spiritual and physical autonomy which, though anti-urban and anti-industrialization, hints at Fuller's taking growthful and propagative advantage of nature's universal patternings.

2. Main quotations in this chapter, "The Formative Years," are extracted from a long biographical letter written by Fuller to the author in 1955. Complete text published in *Architectural Design* (London), July, 1961.

3. James Monroe Hewlett (1869–1941): President, Architectural League, New York 1920–21; President, Society of Mural Painters 1922; Vice-President and Fellow American Institute of Architects 1928; Director, American Academy in Rome 1932–35. Murals include ceiling of Grand Central Terminal, New York City, many stage designs in New York for Metropolitan Opera, etc.

4. The peak year of U.S. building was 1925. Of 572,000 single-family dwellings produced then, only 270 had any interior plumbing. Less than 4 per cent were erected with union labor, less than 2 per cent architect designed. The current shortage was estimated at around 6,000,000 minimal standard dwellings.

5. 4D essays were incorporated in R. B. Fuller, "4D Timelock" (see Bibliography). Fuller's use of 4D as a symbol makes reference to "time" in relativity theory, as a (4th) extension of physical dimension. But latent connotations go further; during this period Fuller seemed preoccupied with time accounting, and conducted a number of experiments in rearranging his work/sleep schedules, etc.

6. Fuller also drew up, at this time, his "Universal Requirements of a Scientific Dwelling Facility" check list. Begun as a control schedule for the Dymaxion House, this has been considerably amplified over the years. Exhaustively detailed, in accordance with his maxim that "in the adequate statement of a problem lies its solution," this document attempts to list every requirement, and meet most contingencies, likely to occur to man in relation to shelter. Also dealt with are the step-by-step design and prototype procedures and the industrial logistics which he saw as required for its implementation. For the latest version, published in 1960, see Bibliography.

7. P. R. Banham, *Theory and Design in the First Machine Age*, London, 1960, pp. 323–26, says, referring to the Dymaxion House, ". . . had it been built, [it] would have rendered *Les Heures Claires* [Le Corbusier's design of 1930], for instance, technically obsolete before design had even begun."

8. Arthur Drexler, in his book, *Ludwig Mies van der Rohe* (New York: George Braziller, Inc., 1960), gives a clue to this when he says that "Mies builds as if technology means only post and lintel construction," pp. 9–10.

9. Though aircraft production rose to 2,000 planes in 1927, and the first passenger airline service in the United States opened between New York and Boston, the lightweight alloy aircraft construction implied in the house was not in general mass production in the United States. Junkers had used metal-stressed skin surfaces, with box-spar construction since 1919; and the 1920 Short "Silver Streak" had duralumin fuselage and wings, but the major production innovation of 1927 was the Lockheed "Vega"—wooden wings, and stressed skin wood fuselage, but of advanced streamline shaping.

10. Quotations of Fuller in this chapter are taken from various letters written during World War II.

11. For expansion of Energy formulation, see World Energy Map (plate 31).

12. The four illustrations in plate 35 are given as reproduced by John J. Grebe, Director of Nuclear and Basic Research, Dow Chemical Company, in his paper on "A Periodic Table for Fundamental Particles," delivered before the New York Academy of Sciences, in which he cites Fuller's work: "These models could represent the structure of the so-called elemental particles mathematically, although not necessarily physically—too little is known to say that. However, it does seem as if these successive layers are significant in the properties—particularly the slow neutron cross-sections—of isotopes, from the smallest nuclear masses to those of the 26th shell, and including both lead and bismuth. . . ."

13. In the 19th century, van't Hoff suggested that all inorganic chemical structures were tetrahedronally configured invertexial linkage. Linus Pauling's X-ray diffraction analyses of 1932 showed omnitetrahedronal configuration interlinkages of gravitational centers of compounded atoms in all metals analyzed. Lord Kelvin, and later, A. Graham Bell, empirically used tetra units as building blocks in structural systems. For diagrams of tetra valency bond, see: G. S. Christiansen and P. H. Garrett, *Structure and Change* (San Francisco: W. H. Freeman & Co., 1960).

14. The term "geodesics" was first used by Hertz, the discoverer of electro-magnetic waves. It was used mathematically by Einstein and Ryman. Fuller defines geodesics as the most economical relationship between a plurality of points or events. Minkowski suggested that the laws of nature may find their most perfect expression in statements about intrinsic topological relations between world lines (geodesics) in some fairly general continuum.

15. Prior to Fuller, geodesic structure was mainly applied only in approximately single curvature structures—as conic (masts), hyper-

bolic (cage masts), cylindrical and elliptical (airframes) **spiraling**
and in lamella roofs. Fuller's geodesics are inherently compound
curvatures, i.e., finite systems. It was unknown mathematically, before energetic/synergetic geometry that any modular frequency of a
symmetrical subdivision of spherical or linear tetrahedrons, octahedrons or icosahedrons provides spring points for geodesic 3-way
grid interactions.

16. A. N. Whitehead, as quoted by Fuller in "The Comprehensive
Man," *Northwest Review*, Spring, 1959.

17. A striking aspect of Fuller's system is that many of its procedures may be conceptually modeled through the employment of
his Energetic Synergetic Geometry. In the trend toward modelability
evident in current scientific development (e.g., in systems simulation,
modelable analogies of whole systems, etc.), this geometry has received a number of citations of congruence with observed behaviors
in many fields. Confirmation of its alignment with structural dis-
coveries, particularly evident since the increased use of electron
microscopy, has occurred in the study of virus and protein mole-
cules as well as fundamental particles. (See, for instance, "Drug
Against a Virus," *Time* magazine, February 16, 1962, p. 50, and
"Virus, a Triumph and a Photograph," New York *Herald Tribune*,
February 6, 1962, pp. 1 ff., as well as note 12, *supra*.) Certain of the
diagrams and conceptual hypotheses employed in mathematical
analysis in the social sciences (e.g., "radex," "circumplex" figures,
and others) show parallel similarities as yet not fully realized. (For
discussion of radex and circumplex, see: P. F. Lazarsfeld, ed., *Mathematical Thinking in Social Sciences* (Glencoe, Illinois: Free Press,
1954.) This rational "all energy behavior accounting" mathematical
tool has recently been further developed by Fuller in a series of
papers called "Omni-directional Halo." These new insights extend
and amplify the postulates of the geometry into the area of a more
generalized epistemology, in a manner which provides a formidable
intellectual apparatus for the elucidation and reduction of complex
phenomenon relationships.

Biographical Chronology

1895	Born July 12, in Milton, Massachusetts
1904–13	Student at Milton Academy
1913–15	Harvard University
1914	Apprentice machine fitter, Richards, Atkinson and Haserick
1915–17	Various positions, Armour and Company, New York City
1917	United States Navy July 12th, married Anne Hewlett
1919	Discharged as lieutenant, United States Navy, at end of World War I
1919–21	Assistant Export Manager, Armour and Company, New York City
1922	Sales Manager, Kelly-Springfield Truck Company
1922–27	President, Stockade Building System
1927–32	Founder and President, 4-D Company, Chicago
1930	Assistant Director of Research, Pierce Foundation
1932–35	Founder, Director, Chief Engineer, Dymaxion Corporation, Bridgeport, Connecticut
1936–38	Assistant to Director, Research and Development, Phelps Dodge Corporation
1938–40	Technical Consultant, *Fortune* magazine
1941–42	Vice-president, Chief Engineer, Dymaxion Company, Inc., Delaware
1942–44	Chief Mechanical Engineer, Board of Economic Welfare. Special Assistant to Director, Foreign Economic Administration
1944–46	Chairman of the Board and Administrative Engineer, Dymaxion Dwelling Machines
1952	Award of Merit, New York Chapter of the American Institute of Architects
1954	Award of Merit, United States Marine Corps
1954–57	Gran Premio, Triennale di Milano, Italy
1955	Centennial Award, Michigan State University
1955–59	President, Synergetics, Inc., Raleigh, North Carolina
1958	Gold Medal Scarab, National Architectural Society
1960	Gold Medal, Philadelphia Chapter of the American Institute of Architects
1960	Frank P. Brown Medal, Franklin Institute
1962	Charles Eliot Norton Professor of Poetry, Harvard University, Cambridge, Massachusetts

Currently:

Chairman of the Board of Trustees of Fuller Research Foundation

President, Geodesics, Inc., Raleigh, North Carolina

President, Plydomes, Inc., Des Moines, Iowa

Research Professor of Generalized Design Science Exploration, Department of Design, Southern Illinois University

Visiting Professorships have been held by Fuller at over 110 American universities and colleges

Life Memberships:

Benjamin Franklin Fellow, Royal Society of Arts, England, 1960

Fellow of the American Association for the Advancement of Science

Honorary Member of the American Institute of Architects

1. *World Town Plan, 1927. Fuller's caption reads: "26 per cent of earth's surface is dry land. 85 per cent of all earth's dry land is here shown. 86 per cent of all dry land shown is above the equator. The whole of the human family could stand on Bermuda. All crowded into England they would have 750 square feet each. 'United we stand, divided we fall' is correct mentally and spiritually, but fallacious physically or materially. 2,000,000,000 new homes will be required in next 80 years."*

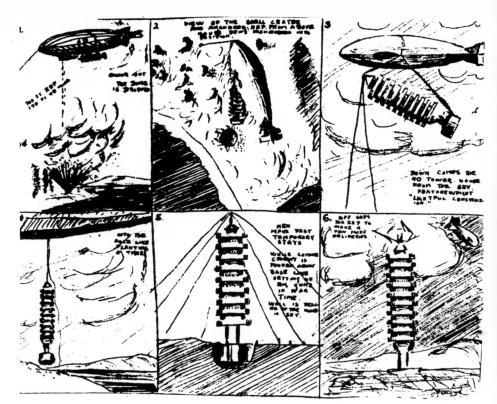

2. *Ten Deck Building, 1927. Airborne by dirigible. Sketch: 1. 700-foot Zep (dirigible), 190-foot 4-D house, anchor out, the bomb is dropped. 2. View of the shell crater and anchored Zep from above; house being maneuvered into position. 3. Down comes the 4-D tower house from the sky, featherweight "lightful construction." 4. Into the hole like planting a tree. 5. Men make fast temporary stays while cement is poured above base, like setting of big guns in wartime. 6. Off goes the Zep to make a few more deliveries.*

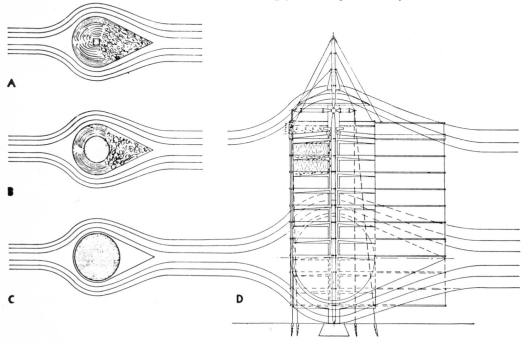

3. *Ten Deck Building. Heat losses of buildings being proportional to air drag, Fuller's diagrams show air current effects of (A) cube, (B) cylinder, (C) streamlined unit, and underlined, by relative size and areas of turbulence, the proportional resistance of these units. This demonstrates efficiency of windshield in reducing drag—heat loss.*

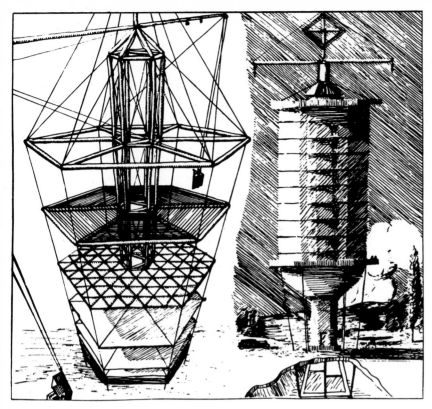

4. *Variation of the Ten Deck Building. Construction details
    (left) and general appearance (right).*

5. *Ten Deck Building. Model, with aerodynamic shield.*

6. *Dymaxion House. Model, 1927.*

7. *Dymaxion House. Model. House parts in shipping order.*

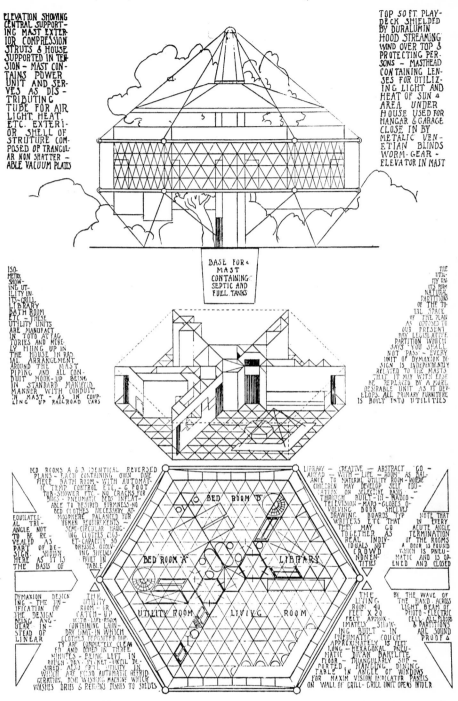

PLAN - ISOMETRIC - AND - ELEVATION OF A MINIMUM DYMAXION HOME

8. *Dymaxion House. Schematic drawing and inventory of functions.*

9. *Dymaxion bathroom. Patent drawing for 1937 version.*

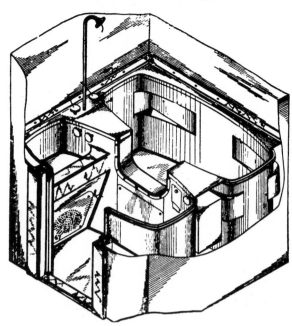

10. *Dymaxion bathroom. Complete unit, weight 420 pounds.*

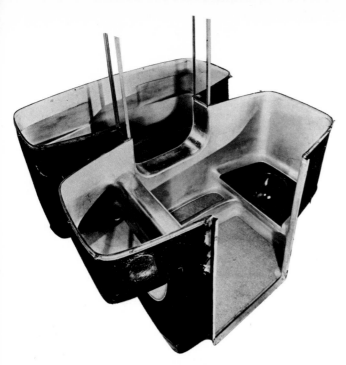

11.   *Dymaxion bathroom unit. 1937 version. Interior.*

12.   *Mechanical Wing, 1940. Drawing.*

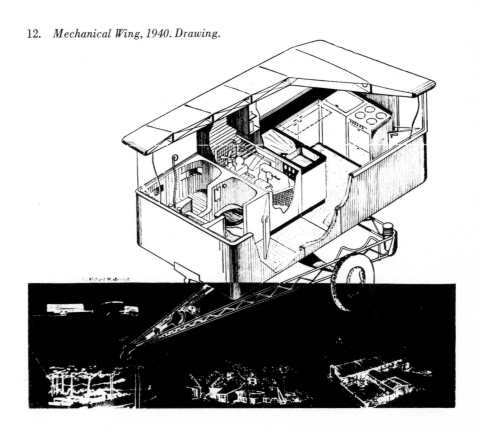

13. *Twin Dymaxion Deployment unit, 1940.*

14. *Twin Dymaxion Deployment unit. Plan.*

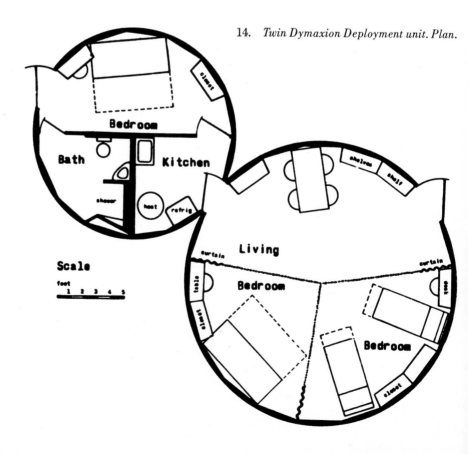

17. *Dymaxion Deployment unit.*
     Interior view of assembly.

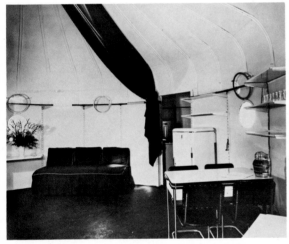

15. *Dymaxion Deployment unit. Interior, view*
     of kitchen, bath, and bedroom unit.

16. *Dymaxion Deployment unit. Exterior assembly.*

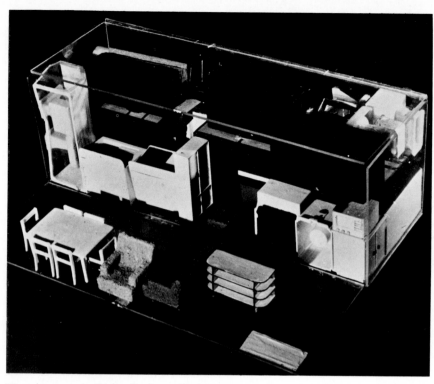

18. *Autonomous Living Package. Model, 1949,*
     with space registry of six face loads (one face open).

19. *Autonomous Living Package.*
     Model (partially open).

20. *Autonomous Living Package.*
     Model (fully open).

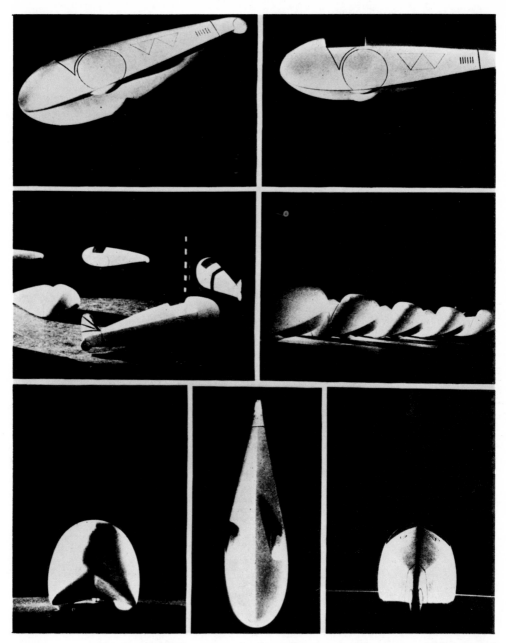

21. *Land and Air maneuvering Dymaxion jet-stilt, 4-D transport, 1927. Inverted V bottom provides air-keel speed as well as tail-lift (for speeds over 50 mph).*

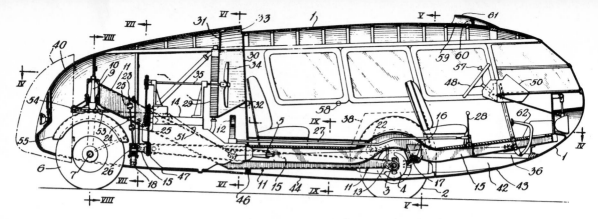

22. *Dymaxion car. Patent drawing filed 1933.*

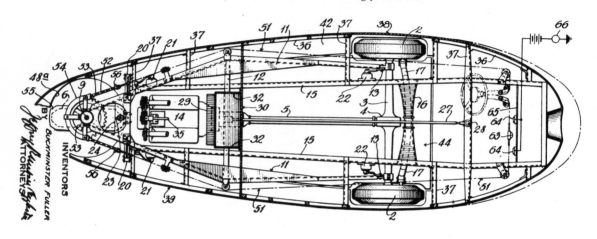

23. *Dymaxion car No. 3, 1934.*

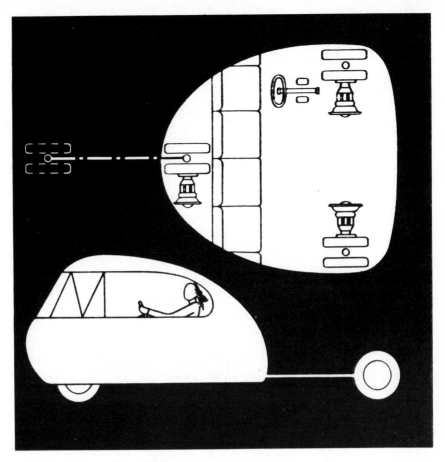

24. *Dymaxion car No. 4, 1948.*

25.   *Wichita House, 1946. Finished shell state with empty packing cylinder at left.*

26.   *Wichita House. Model. Interior.*

27.   *Wichita House. Atmospheric field flow studies.*

28.   *Wichita House. Living room interior.*

29.   *Wichita House. Parts stacked for shipping.*

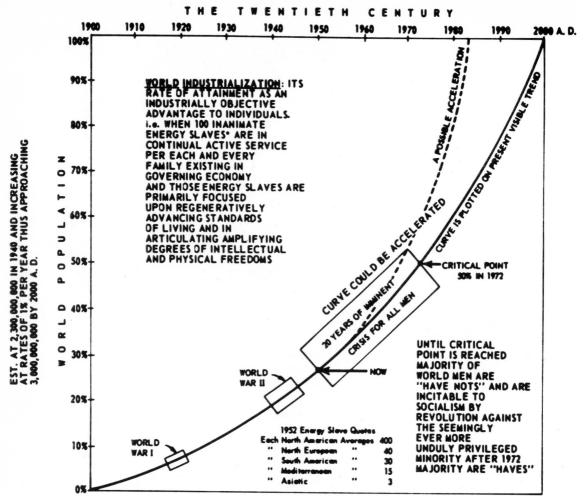

The chart contains:

THE TWENTIETH CENTURY

WORLD POPULATION

EST. AT 2,300,000,000 IN 1940 AND INCREASING AT RATES OF 1% PER YEAR THUS APPROACHING 3,600,000,000 BY 2000 A.D.

WORLD INDUSTRIALIZATION: ITS RATE OF ATTAINMENT AS AN INDUSTRIALLY OBJECTIVE ADVANTAGE TO INDIVIDUALS. i.e. WHEN 100 INANIMATE ENERGY SLAVES° ARE IN CONTINUAL ACTIVE SERVICE PER EACH AND EVERY FAMILY EXISTING IN GOVERNING ECONOMY AND THOSE ENERGY SLAVES ARE PRIMARILY FOCUSED UPON REGENERATIVELY ADVANCING STANDARDS OF LIVING AND IN ARTICULATING AMPLIFYING DEGREES OF INTELLECTUAL AND PHYSICAL FREEDOMS

A POSSIBLE ACCELERATION

CURVE IS PLOTTED ON PRESENT VISIBLE TREND

CURVE COULD BE ACCELERATED

20 YEARS OF IMMINENT CRISIS FOR ALL MEN

CRITICAL POINT 50% IN 1972

NOW

WORLD WAR II

WORLD WAR I

UNTIL CRITICAL POINT IS REACHED MAJORITY OF WORLD MEN ARE "HAVE NOTS" AND ARE INCITABLE TO SOCIALISM BY REVOLUTION AGAINST THE SEEMINGLY EVER MORE UNDULY PRIVILEGED MINORITY AFTER 1972 MAJORITY ARE "HAVES"

1952 Energy Slave Quotas
Each North American Averages 400
" North European " 40
" South American " 30
" Mediterranean " 15
" Asiatic " 3

30. *World Industrialization chart, 1952.*

31. *World Energy Map, 1940. Dymaxion projection of spherical world as a flat surface with no visible distortion. All openings in the stretched-out earth "skin" occur in the one and continuous ocean. This allows the particular arrangement of linked-together continental masses without breaks in their contours, surrounded by "their" oceans. Fourteen segments can be assembled in various combinations as three-dimensional approximation of a globe. The curved arrangements of population symbols indicate major population concentrations. Each related dot equals 1 per cent of the world's inanimate power, called "energy slaves." Energy slaves are determined as follows: In an 8-hour day, one man can do approximately 150,000 foot-pounds of work (the energy required to lift one pound one foot vertically). Consumption of mineral and water energy in 1950 is estimated at 80⅕ quintillion foot-pounds. Man's efficiency converts only a rough 4 per cent of these into work, or about 3⅕ quintillion foot-pounds. Dividing this by 250 work days' (one year) energy output of one man (37½ million foot-pounds), the result is 85½ billion man-year equivalents of work done by machines and structures. These equivalents are called "energy slaves."*

There are about 38 energy slaves per capita, but:

	world population	world energy slaves	per capita energy slaves
Asia	50%	3%	2
Europe	24%	17%	27
Africa	12%	4%	13
North America	8%	73%	347
South America	4%	3%	28
Central America	1%	0%	0
All others	1%	0%	0

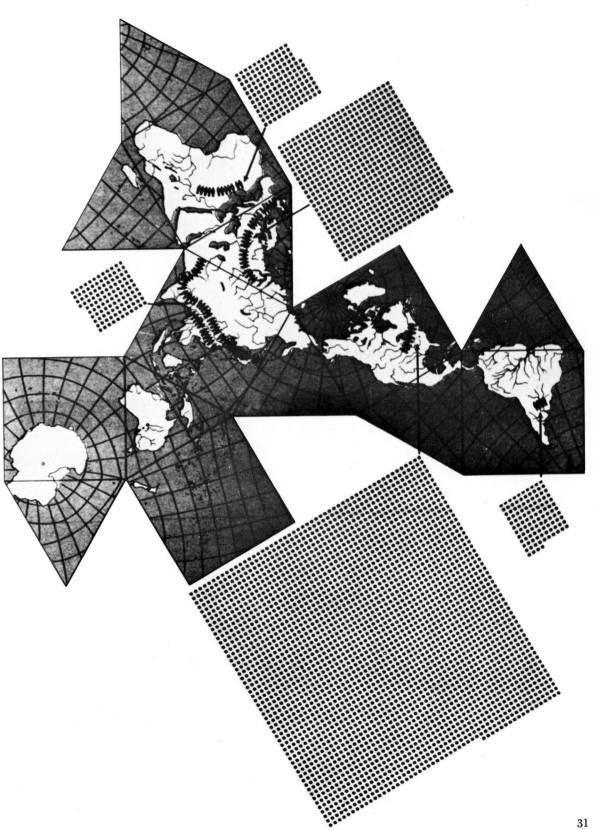

32. *Dymaxion Air Ocean World Map, 1954.*

33. *Minni-Earth Sphere, Cornell University, 1952. Early development of Geoscope project.*

34. *Energetic and Synergetic Geometry. Models of closest packing of spheres.*

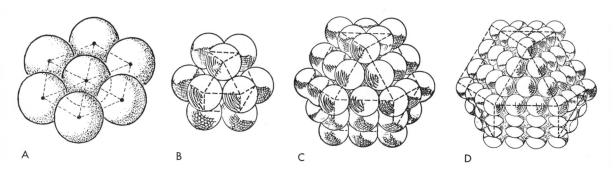

A   B   C   D

35. *Energetic and Synergetic Geometry. Drawing of closest packing of spheres. (A) Two-dimensional closest packing of spheres around a nucleus forms regular hexagonal patterns. Spheres can be considered as expanded vertexes of the equilateral triangles. (B) Omnidirectional closest packing. Twelve balls in first layer surrounding nucleus. (C) Omnidirectional closest packing. Forty-two balls in second layer surrounding nucleus. (D) Omnidirectional closest packing. Ninety-two balls in third surrounding layer. Thus, one ball: nucleus; 12 balls: 1st layer (radius 1); 42 balls: 2nd layer (radius 2); 92 balls: 3rd layer (radius 3); and so forth. Subtract common 2 from each total, then divide by 10; the remaining numbers (1, 4, 9, etc.) are the squares of radii. The number of balls in any layer equals (radius^2 × 10)+2.*

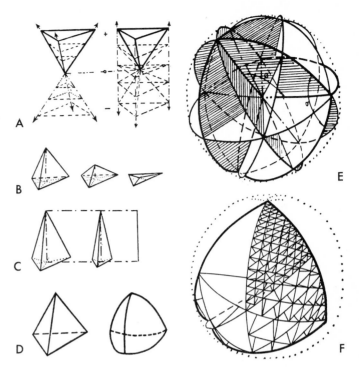

A

B

C

D

E

F

36. *Energetic and Synergetic Geometry: (A) The tetrahedron is minimum and therefore basic structural system; all structure is a complex of tetrahedroxel transformations. (B) Tetrahedrons are seemingly unique because they may be turned inside out and pass through zero phases of other transformations. (C) A triangle (truss) is a tetrahedron of zero phase altitude. A line is a tetrahedron of zero phase base. A point is a tetrahedron of combined zero phase of both altitude and base. (D) In addition to its four facets a tetrahedron has four vertexes and six edges. Its edges may be "straight" or "visible" arcs. (E) The regular six-chord-edged tetrahedron encloses (defines) the minimum volume with the most surface of all geometric polyhedrons or structural systems; whereas sphere encloses most volume with least surface and the minimum sphere-defining structure is the regular six-great-circle-arc-edged tetrahedron of 109°28′ central angles and 120° surface angles. As there may be no absolute division of energetic universe into isolated or non-communicable parts, there is no absolute enclosed surface or absolutely enclosed volume; therefore, no true or absolutely defined simultaneous surface sphere integrity. Therefore, a sphere is a polyhedron of invisible plurality of trussed facets ("trussed" because all polygons are reducible to triangles or trusses and are further irreducible) and trusses are therefore basic polygons. Infinite polyhedron is infinitely faceted by basic trusses.*

37. *Energetic and Synergetic Geometry. Geometrical development of geodesics. (A) Sphere. (B) Tetrahedron. (C) Octahedron. (D) Icosahedron. (E) Icosahedron exploded onto sphere. (F) Geodesic grid.*

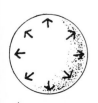

A

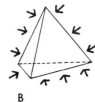

B

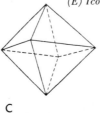

C

D

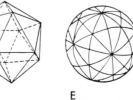

E

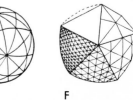

F

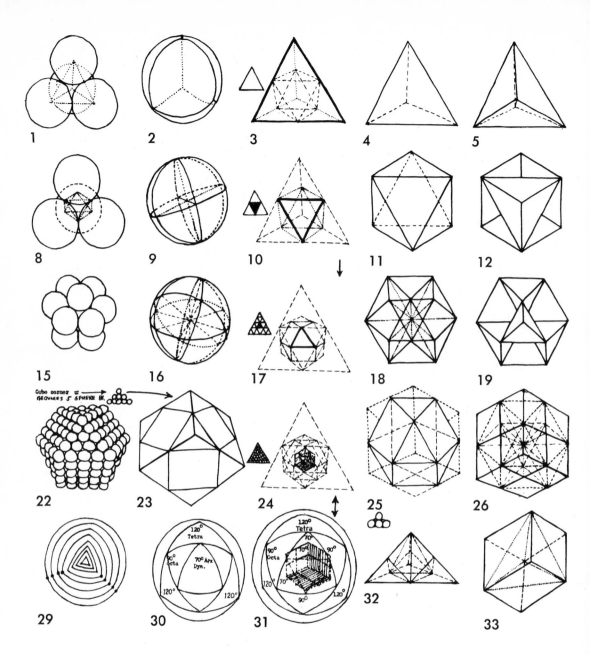

1

2

3

4

5

8

9

10

11

12

15

16

17

18

19

Cube corner = REQUIRES 5 SPHERE ETC.

22

23

24

25

26

29

30

31

32

33

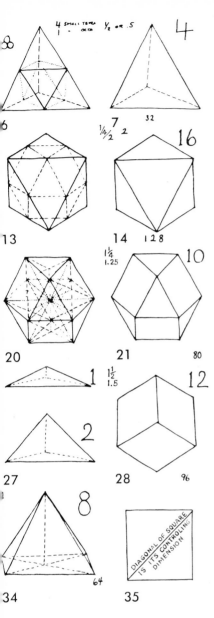

1. TETRAHEDRON. Convergently or compressively organized plurality of spherical nuclei. Exterior ballistics, 2 visible, 2 invisible orbits.

2. Divergently organized single sphere—interior compression—exterior tension, subdivided by great circles; absolute of 2nd orbit—maximum volume with minimum surface. Correct first subdivision of spherical surface one dimension into four. Weds ⅓ of unity of vertexes to ¼ of unity of surface with 6 arc segments and 4 vertexes.

3. EXTERIOR. Position in super tetrahedron convergent phase of vectors. All vertexes are spherical centers. All angles are 60°. Tetrahedron has octahedron center.

4. Tensed INTERIOR geometric vector construction in equilibrium. Minimum volume with maximum surface. 4 equal planes perpendicular to separate axis=4 dimensions.

5. Absolute convergence first orbit. No volume, exterior compression. Internal tension. 60° x 35° x 110° pyramids. 4 parts.

6. Divergent components of octave subdivision. 4 small tetra, 1 small octa.

7. Convergent and divergent unit and fractional values in high-low octaves. ½ or .5.

8. OCTAHEDRON. Tensive core.

9. Interlocked vectors of 8 tetrahedrons. 3 axes.

10. Center of octahedron is dymaxion.

11. Eight equiangular equilateral surface triangles.

12. Right components are 60° triangle base, 45° x 90° pyramids.

13. Octahedron has dymaxion center.

14. Octahedron surface.

15. DYMAXION. 12 spheres surrounding 1, all in tangency. Outer spheres 5 contacts each. Center sphere, 12.

16. 6 axes (4 dimensions). Fully divergent vector system with unit tetra and octa vertex center.

17. Center of octahedron is dymaxion.

18. Dymaxion only solid with natural center and radius identical with all dimensions. Monometer.

19. Dymaxion as a uniform vector field diaphragm converting or compounding 2-and-3 values. Unit cube has no center of its own.

20. Dymaxion is comprehensive to tetra and octahedrons and is the decimal octave.

21. 10 with diameter x unity; 80 with radius or edge x unity.

22. This most compact spherical agglomeration expands to infinity; new nucleus every 4 orbits.

23. CUBE.

24. Cube-octave group within dymaxion center is not a cube within dymaxion but an octave reduction. Cubes do not center singly. Only do so as octave collection (see figures 26 and 33). 8 cube core under octahedron face.

25. Cube corners borrowed from neighboring nuclei in third orbit. Cube corners=⅛ octahedron.

26. Octave of cubes' center—cube collection has common center with dymaxion—9 axes.

27. *1)* 60° triangle base x 35° x 110° (approx.). Pyramid equal ¼ of tetrahedron formed on center tetrahedron. Adopted as VOLUMETRIC UNITY. *2)* 60° triangle base x 45° x 90° has volume of 2.

28. Icosahedron of unit exterior measure has octave values of 9 or 72, which are natural zeroes.

29. Concentric spherical triangles. 180°— to 60°+ great circle is absolute triangle.

30. Icosahedron not in this bisection of triangles sequence. 71°=Icosahedron's vertex.

31. 8 cube core under octahedron face.

32. 60° triangle base 45° x 90° pyramid has tetra at center +6 of next lower octave 60 x 45 x 90 pyramids.

33. Individual cube has tetrahedron at its center.

34. 60° triangle faced square-based pyramid equaling ½ an octahedron has volume of 8.

35. Unity = 2 ∴ sides of square = √1

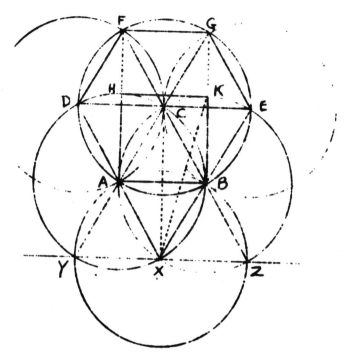

39. *Energetic and Synergetic Geometry. The square is developed from a point on a line by use of one divider angle only. Two equilateral triangles, XYA and XBZ are formed on the baseline YZ, flanking a point X. These triangles trisect the 180° angle YXZ into three 60° angle, YXA, AXB, and BXZ. The 180° angle YXZ next is bisected from the second orbit construction point C, equidistant from A and B. CX also bisects angle AXB into 30° angles AXC and CXB. From second orbit base DCE, equidistant and parallel to YXZ, F and G are developed equidistant from each other and from D, C, and E. Parallel lines FA and GB intersect arcs DC and CE at H and K respectively and therefore HKBA is a square. (From this we also know that ABK is 90° and ABX is 60° divided by 150°; and because KBX is an isosceles triangle, the angles XKB and KXB are 15° each. KX bisects angle CXB.)*

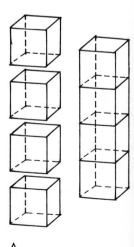

40. *Tensegrity. (A) Two stacks of columns of tubes. (B) One stack (left) contains the positive tetrahedrons; the other (right) contains the negative tetrahedrons. (C) We put a steel sphere at CG of cube which is also CG of tetrahedron and run steel tubes from CG to four corners of WXYZ of negative tetrahedron. Every tetrahedron's center of gravity (CG) has four radials from CG to the four corners of the tetrahedron. (D) The junction between two tetrahedrons. The system is nonredundant, a basic discontinuous compression, continuous tension structure. Ball joints CG^1 and CG^2 are pulled toward each other by vertical tension stay, thus thrusting universally jointed legs outward, their outward thrust being stably restrained by finite sling closure. Y, X, Z, W. (E) A stack of CG radial tube tetrahedron struts with horizontal (approximate) tension slings and vertical tension guys and diagonal tension edges of the four superimposed tetrahedrons which, because of the horizontal slings, cannot come any closer to one another and because of their vertical guys cannot get any further away from one another, and therefore comprise a stable relationship.*

A

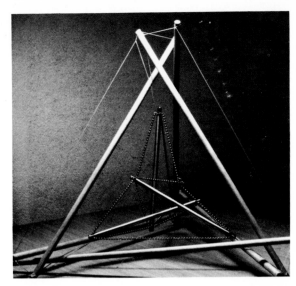

41. *Four-strut tetra tensegrity suspended as central angles of 6-strut (peripheral) tensegrity.*

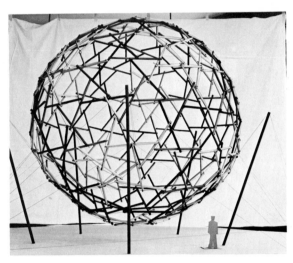

42. *270-strut model for 42-foot-diameter sphere, University of Minnesota, 1953.*

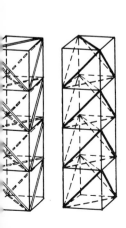

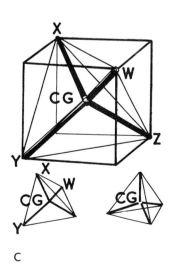

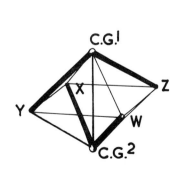

C

D

E

43. *Tensegrity model by Kenneth Snelson. Exhibited at 1959 Museum of Modern Art showing of Fuller projects.*
(Photo: Courtesy of the Museum of Modern Art, New York.)

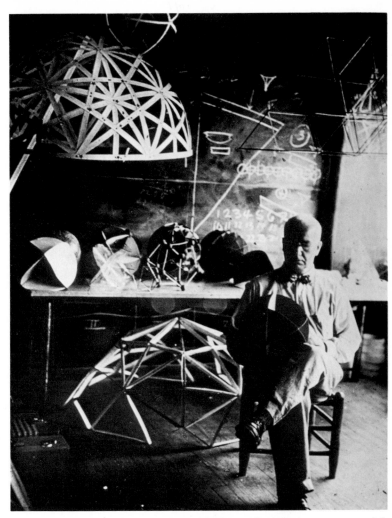

44.   *Fuller with geodesic structure models*
at Black Mountain College, 1947.

45.   *Tensegrity sphere of 8-foot diameter, Southern Illinois*
University, 1959. Adaptable as environment-control structure.

46. *"Hex-pent" channel dome, Institute of Design, Chicago, 1948. 14-foot diameter; weight, 25 pounds.*

47. *Tension Integrity Mast, 1949. Illustrates use of discontinuous compression and continuous tension.*

48. *"Necklace" geodesic, Black Mountain College, 1949. 14-foot diameter, weight 50 pounds. This dome had continuous internal cable, enabling it to be folded into a package (similar to later "seed-pod" and "aspension" structures).*

49.   *Automatic Cotton Mill, geodesic and octet truss, North Carolina State College, 1952. Model.*

50. *Automatic Cotton Mill. Model seen from above.*

51. *Automatic Cotton Mill. Diagram showing design of central service mast with elevator, three-way-truss floor and enclosing shell.*

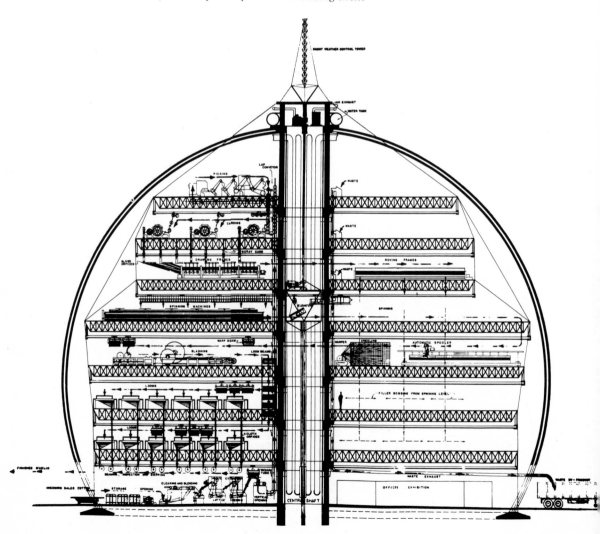

52. *Egg-crate geodesic structure, New York, 1952. 6-foot diameter; weight, 10 pounds.*
Illustrates use of two-way compression and one-way tension.

53. *Dynamic dome, University of Michigan, 1952. Weight, 30 pounds.*

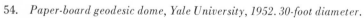

54. *Paper-board geodesic dome, Yale University, 1952. 30-foot diameter.*

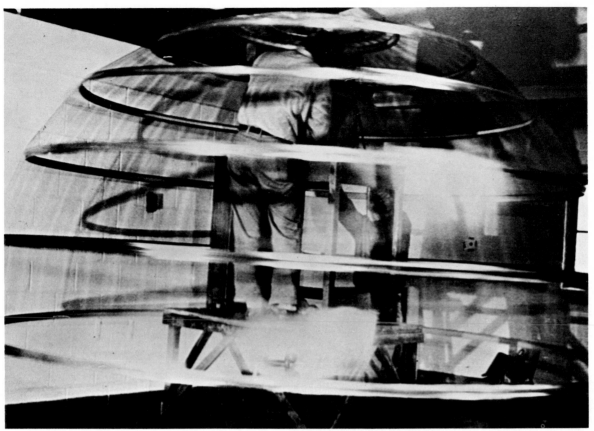

55.   *Dynamic dome in motion. Space is controlled by revolving openwork skin fast enough to give a rainshed, showing how large areas can be covered by dynamic shaping through mechanical or electronic means. The "dynamic dome," like the "seed-pod" and "aspension" structures, is a development study in dynamic structures, also envisaged to be able to be parachuted, air-dropped or rocketed to inaccessible locations.*

56. *"Seed-pod" structure (self-erecting), Washington University, 1955. 36-foot diameter. Detail of folded dome, forming a pack 9 feet long, 3 feet in diameter, and weighing 300 pounds.*

57. *"Seed-pod" structure. Dome begins expansion. Force for erection of the dome is provided by compressed nitrogen in valves at each of the 30 tripod vertexes.*

58. *"Seed-pod" structure. Dome erect, composed of 30 inwardly folding tripod assemblies, restrained at the limit of their open position by interconnecting cables to tripod foot, which is a ball-and-socket joint.*

59. *Restaurant dome at Woods Hole, Massachusetts, 1954. 54-foot diameter; weight, 6,000 pounds. It is made of 1" x 8" and 2" x 3" wood members infilled with clear plastic.*

60. *Ford Rotunda Building, Ford River Rouge Plant,*
    Dearborn, Michigan, 1953. Dome partially completed.

61. *Ford Rotunda Building. Exterior view.*

62.   *Ford Rotunda Building. View of completed dome.*

63.   *Ford Rotunda Building.*
      Octahedrons assembled.

65. *Fuller witnesses successful completion of first airlift delivery of U.S. Marine Corps shelter in 1954.*

64. *Ford Rotunda Building. Detail of dome as final sheets of Fiberglas polyester resin skin are applied to the outside.*

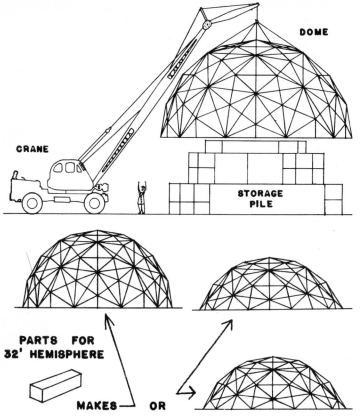

DOME

CRANE

STORAGE
PILE

PARTS FOR
32' HEMISPHERE

MAKES — OR

66. *Marine Corps standard dome package, 1954. Possible
variations of 32-foot hemisphere.*

67. *Marines carry 36-foot-diameter dome.*

68. *Milan Triennale paper-board dome, 1954. Detail of interior. The dome is made of corrugated Kraft paper-board sheet on which cuts, folds, and assembly instructions are printed in one continuous operation. Sheet units are folded, stapled, and taped together on site using minimum tools.*

69. *Milan Triennale paper-board dome. Night view. 36-foot diameter.*

70. *Milan Triennale paper-board dome. View of dome in exhibition grounds.*

71. *Plastic Radome, Mount Washington, 1954. No metal or wood parts; ¾ sphere; weight, 3,000 pounds. This dome withstood 200 mph winds, hurricane force, for two years without damage. (It is similar to domes now in use across the Arctic radar line.)*

72. *Radome, 1955. Night view. ¾ sphere, 55-foot diameter.*

73. *"Pinecone" plywood sheet dome, Cornell University, 1957. 40-foot diameter. Similar low-cost structures have been developed through other pilot studies and are now produced commercially.*

74. *United States Pavilion at World Trades Fair, Kabul, Afghanistan, 1956.*

75. *Plywood dome, test erected in Hartford, Iowa, 1957, for use as chapel in Korea. 39-foot diameter. Made of 135 quarter-inch plywood sheets with plasticized coating, predrilled for bolting and sealed with plastic tape. Openings are clear plastic.*

76. *Peasedome, fabricated by Pease Woodwork Company, Ohio, 26-foot diameter, wood frame, plywood sheet dome.*

77.   *Kaiser Aluminum Dome, Honolulu, Hawaii, 1957. 145-foot diameter. Erected in 22 hours.*

78.   *Kaiser Aluminum Dome. Interior.*

79. *"Indhlu" Dome, University of Natal, South Africa, seminar project, 1958. Made of corrugated aluminum, 18.8-foot diameter; weight, 200 pounds; 12 feet high at center. Mass housing prototype.*

80.   *Union Tank Car Company Dome, Baton Rouge, Louisiana, 1958–59. Diameter, 384 feet; 120 feet high at center.*
    Made of 321 hexagonal steel panels, each folded and dimensionally braced with tubes and rods.

81. *Union Tank Car Comany Dome, Baton Rouge. 100-foot-diameter interior dome which houses the administrative control center.*

82. *"Golden Dome," Kaiser Aluminum Dome, Moscow, 1959. 200-foot diameter. Fuller is shown in front of this dome which housed part of the United States exhibit.*

84. *Aluminum lattice dome, American Society of Metals
Headquarters Building, Ohio, 1959. Diameter, 250 feet.
(Designed along Fuller's principles by T. C. Howard.)
The dome was intended to be symbolic. There are no
infilled panels or enclosing skin.*

83. *Museum of Modern Art (N.Y.) 1959 Fuller exhibition,
showing 36-foot tensegrity mast of aluminum tube and
monel rods, built by Shoji Sadao and Edison Price.
Octet-truss structure, 100 feet long, 35 feet wide,
cantilevered 60 feet one way and 40 feet the other,
fabricated from 2-inch aluminum tubes (from Aluminium
Canada) by North American Aviation Company: plastic
Radome, loaned by Lincoln Laboratory, M.I.T., 55-foot
diameter. (Photo: Courtesy of the Museum of Modern Art,
New York, by Alexandre Georges.)*

85. *St. Louis "Climatron," Missouri Botanical Garden, 1960.*
Diameter 175 feet, 70 feet high at center with clear
plastic infill panels. Interior.

86. *St. Louis "Climatron." Exterior.*

87. *Air deliverable theater, Ford Motor Company, Jam Handy Tractor Division, 1960. Diameter, 140 feet; aluminum frame; black nylon cover. The dome can be assembled ready for use in 1½ hours.*

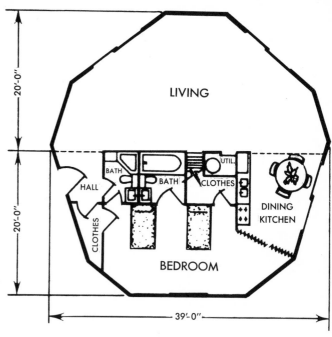

LIVING

BATH
BATH
UTIL.
CLOTHES

HALL

CLOTHES

DINING
KITCHEN

BEDROOM

20'-0"

20'-0"

39'-0"

88.   *Fuller's home. Plan.*

89.   *Buckminster Fuller's home dome, Carbondale, Illinois, 1960. The dome is a standard*
production structure of Peasedomes, Inc. 39-foot diameter, wood frame, plywood panel construction.

90. *Fuller's home. Interior showing living area. Stairway to library deck above on right.*

91. *Prestressed concrete dome for Denver Fraternity House, 1960. 55-foot diameter. Interior detail. (Architect in charge was Tom Moore.)*

92. *Monsanto "Geospace" dome, 1961. A mass-produced 22-foot-diameter dome; yielding 350 square feet usable floor space, 3,000 cubic feet storage volume; weight, 350 pounds. Panels are machine cut from ½-inch "Fomecor" board. These domes have been used as emergency housing in Puerto Rico.*

93. *Bamboo dome, Long Beach State College, 1960. 46-foot diameter.*

94.	*Aviary dome, Tampa, Florida, 1959, built for Anheuser Busch by Union Tank Company.*
	99-foot diameter, 20½ feet high, gold anodized aluminum with 2-inch-square mesh.

95.	*Wood River Dome, Illinois, 1960. Union Tank Car Company.*
	Total weight above foundations is 567 tons.

96. *Aspension tensegrity dome, 1961. Model.*

97.   *Aspension tensegrity dome. Detail of model.*

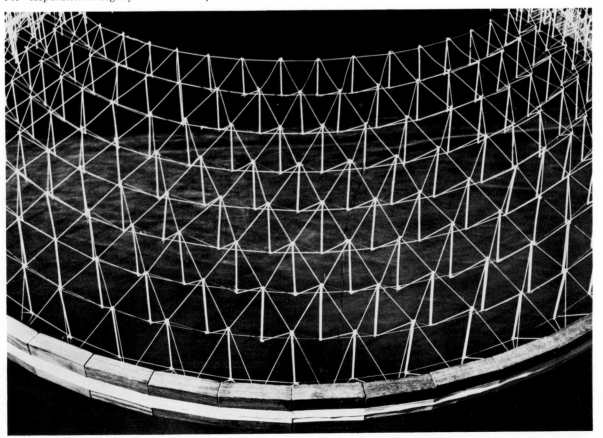

98. *Bamboo tensegrity dome, Calcutta, 1961. Study for low-cost shelter using local material and facilities.*

99. *Basketry tensegrity dome, Southern Illinois University, 1962. 72-foot diameter. This is the first usable reduction to practice of tensegrity structuring, promising a very low-cost environment enclosure. The materials for the prototype shown would cost approximately $500.*

100. *Basketry tensegrity dome, Southern Illinois University, 1962. Detail.*

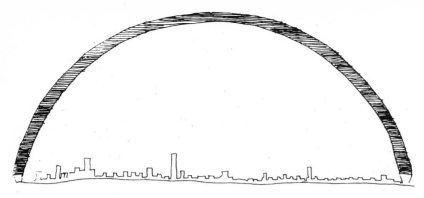

101. *Buckminster Fuller's drawing for a 2-mile hemispherical dome.*

102. *Design for a hemispherical dome 2 miles in diameter. This dome could enclose a large part of New York City, as illustrated. Weighing about 80,000 tons, it could be assembled in 5-ton sections by helicopters in three months and would cost about $200 million dollars. It is believed that the savings to the city in such items as air-conditioning (dome provides its own natural air circulation), street-cleaning, snow removal, and lost man-hours from colds and other respiratory ailments would soon repay initial investment. A synergetic surprise feature of such very large structures is that the thickness of the enclosing shell could be of occupiable dimension—for living not only under but* in *dome covering.*

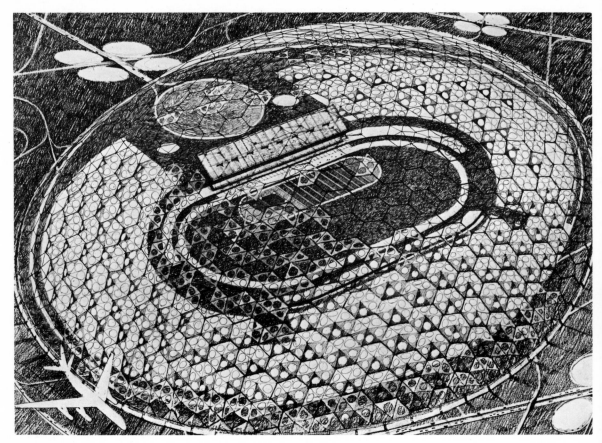

103. *Dome project, 1961. 100-acre span, 450 feet high at center. This dome would be largest roofed structure in the world. It was initially planned as a covering for a raceway and surroundings.*

From a Letter in Answer to an Inquiry by Collier's Reference Service Regarding Fuller's Geometry, October 1959

In 1917 I started exploring for and since then have discovered and have progressively inventoried what probably constitutes the comprehensive, omni-rational, mathematical coordinate system employed by nature throughout all her complementary and accommodatively transforming transactions. I have named the discovered coordinate system Energetic and Synergetic Geometry.

Energetic and Synergetic Geometry embraces all known facets of mathematics. Rather than refuting the bases of presently known Euclidean and Non-Euclidean Hyperbolic and Elliptic geometry, Energetic-Synergetic Geometry identifies the alternative freedoms of prime axiomatic assumption from which the present mathematical bases were selected. All of the axiomatic alternatives are logical. Some result in awkwardness of complex relationship expression. Occurring amongst the alternate axiomatic assumptive freedoms, Energetic-Synergetic Geometry discovers and employs a new set of axioms which seemingly result in sublimely facile expression of hitherto complex relationships . . . as for instance:

Universe is finite.

Local systems are de-finite.

Unity is a complex, volumetric plurality at minimum two.

Unities may be treated as complex star points.

A point is an as-yet-undifferentiated focal star embracing a complex of local events.

For every point in universe there are six uniquely and exclusively operative vectors.

Each vector is reversible having its negative alternate.

Every point may export all or any of its six positive or six negative vectors by importing like numbers.

Each point in universe could be said to have twelve unique and exclusive vectors, but one set of six is operative and its alternate reverse effect set is only potential.

All lines are the most economical vectorial interrelationships of non-simultaneous local event foci.

Potentially straight line relationships require instantaneity or actions in no-time, therefore straight lines are inoperative.

114   All lines are complexedly curved.

The vectorial lines of relationship are always most economical, ergo geodesic.

All geodesic lines weave four dimensionally amongst one another, forever, without ever touching one another.

Potential lines are straight, all realized relationships are geodesic and curved.

All lines ultimately return into close proximity of themselves.

Where all the local vectors are approximately equal, we have a potentially isotropic local vector equilibrium, but the operative vector complex has the inherent qualities of *proximity* and *remoteness* in respect to any locally initiated action ergo a complex of relative velocities of realization lags.

No lines may occupy the same point at the same time.

Whereas none of the geodesic lines of universe touch one another, the lines approach one another, passing successively through regions of most critical proximity, and diverge from one another, passing successively through regions of most innocuous remoteness.

Universe is a non-simultaneously potential vector equilibrium.

All local events of universe may be calculatively anticipated by inaugurating calculation with a local vector equilibrium frame and identifying the disturbance initiating point, direction, and energy of introduced action.

Energetic-Synergetic Geometry's six positive and six negative dimensional reference frames are reinitiated and regenerated in respect to specific local developments and interrelationships of universe.

Arithmetical one dimensionality is identified geometrically with linear, pointal frequency.

Arithmetical two dimensionality is identified geometrically with areal pointal frequency.

Arithmetical six dimensionality is identified geometrically with vectorial system modular frequency relationship.

Arithmetical size dimensionality is identified geometrically with *relative frequency modulation.*

Frequency is multi-cyclic fractionation of unity.

A minimum of two cycles are essential to frequency fractionation.

Angle is sub-cyclic—i.e., fractionation of one cycle.

Angular relationships and magnitudes are sub-cyclic ergo sub-frequency ergo independent of size.

Shape is exclusively angular.

Shape is independent of *size*.

Abstraction means pattern relationship independent of size. Shape being independent of size is abstractable.

Abstractions may be stated in pure principle of relationship.

Abstractions are conceptually shapable.

Different shapes ergo different abstractions are non-simultaneous; but all shapes are de-finite components of integral though non-simultaneous ergo shapeless universe.

There are no indivisible points.

There are no straight lines.

There are no impervious surface continuums.

A "point" is a tetrahedron of negligible altitude and base dimensions.

A "line" is a tetrahedron of negligible base dimension and significant altitude.

A "plane" is a tetrahedron of negligible altitude and significant base dimensionality.

There are no solids, nor particles,—no-things.

The tetrahedron is the lowest common rational denominator of universe. The four unique quanta numbers of each and every fundamental "particle" are the four unique and minimum "stars" of every tetrahedron.

Energetic-Synergetic Geometry does disclose the excruciating awkwardness characterising present-day mathematical treatment of the inter-relationships of the independent scientific disciplines as originally occasioned by their mutual and separate lacks of awareness of the existence of a comprehensive rational coordinating system inherent in nature.

From R. B. Fuller, No More Second Hand God (*Carbondale, Southern Illinois University Press, 1962*)

This coordinate system may be described as an *isotropic vector* system, that is a generalized Avogadro system in which the energy conditions and relative quanta ratios are everywhere the same yet multi-differentiable in local patterning aspects, which aspects are interchangeably emergent without altering the comprehensive energy equilibrium or its unitary totality as implicit in the *Law of Conservation of Energy* by which it is assumed that energy may be neither created nor lost.

The discovered coordinate system is apparently governed by generalized laws, some of whose mathematical equatability I have been allowed not only to discern (as far as I know for the first time by anyone) but also to codify and translate into unique structural realizations. This codification governs the total coordinate abundance ratios of the unique pattern aspect relationships of uniquely irreducible cooperative function aspects of pattern totality.

Discovery of the primary and corollary laws of constantly coordinate relative abundance of pattern function-aspects of totality as an omni-rational regularity governing all local patternings of universe as a minimum-maximum family of complexedly complementary yet uniquely identifiable conceptual function-patterning relationships followed upon intuitive formulations of the seemingly most comprehensive self-querying question I was capable of propounding to myself regarding possible detectable pattern significances accruing to progressive life experience integrations and overlays.

That most comprehensive question was "What do you mean by the word 'universe'?" "If you cannot answer, you had best abandon use of the word 'universe' for it will have no meaning." My intuitively adopted rules for self-questioning and answering were that the answer must be made exclusively from man's experience patterns. I learned many years later that the Nobel physicist, Percy Williams Bridgman, had identified this same rule adopted by Einstein as "operational procedure," subsequently a much abused phrase. My answer (or discard of the word "universe" as a communication tool) was inherent in the rules—"Universe is the aggregate of all consciously apprehended and communicated (to self or relayed to others) experience of man." If my finite answer holds against all specific experience challenges as being comprehensively anticipatory and adequate then *universe is finite*, and all its components *definable*. Each life as we know it is *de*finitive, i.e., consists of a plurality of terminable, ergo definite, experiences, beginning with each awakening and terminating with each surrender to sleep (no man can prove upon awakening that he is the man who he thinks went earlier to sleep, nor that aught else which he thinks he recollects is other than a convincing dream). The intermittent beginnings and endings of conscious experience constitute an aggregate of definitive experiences—and the aggregate is therefore finite.

In the recent movements of historical experience, men as scientists adopted the "law of conservation of energy": as predicated upon the sum total experience of physicists which recalled no contradiction to this hypothesis. They thus accomplished a finite packaging of all physical behaviors of physical universe as predicated also upon the hypothesis that all physical phenomena are entirely energetic.

By embracing all the energetic phenomena of total experience, the scientists secured a synergetic advantage for all energy accounting and prospecting. "Synergy" means "behavior of whole systems unpredicted by the behavior of any of its components or by any sub-array of its components." Corollary to synergy is *the law of the whole system*. Systems are definite as they return upon themselves in a plurality of directions, ergo have concave inwardness and convex outwardness, ergo inherently subdivide universe into mutually exclusive definitive macro and micro entities. *The law of whole system* states that, given the sum of whole system pattern conception, its component behaviors may be differentially discovered and predictably described as required by the already evidenced behavior functions implicit in the aprioridefinitive experience and conceptioning of any given experience-verified system. Thus by the law of whole system as corollary of synergy, the component behaviors of systems may be predictably differentiated as primary and secondary componential sub-divisions of whole system and then progressively isolated and locally reconsidered for further dichotomy.

From R. B. Fuller, Education Automation (*Carbondale, Southern Illinois University Press, 1962*)

My experience is now world-around. During one-third of a century of experimental work, I have been operating on the philosophic premise that all thoughts and all experiences can be translated much further than just into words and abstract thought patterns. I saw that they can be translated into patterns which may be realized in various *physical* projections —by which we can alter the physical environment itself and thereby induce other men to subconsciously alter their ecological patterning. My own conclusion is that man has been given the capability to alter and accelerate the evolutionary transformation of the a priori physical environment—that is, to participate objectively, directly and consciously in universal evolution—and I assume that the great, complex integrity of omni-coordinate and inter-accommodative yet periodically unique and nonsimultaneously cooperative generalized principles, and their myriad of special case realizations, all of which we speak of as universe and may think intuitively of as God is an intellectual invention system which counts on man's employing these capabilities. If he does not do so consciously, events will transpire so that he functions subconsciously in the inexorable evolutionary transformations.

As a consequence of man's having the faculty to apprehend patterns external to himself and the capability of altering those patterns, interesting changes in the conscious relationship of man to universe are now multiplying in evidence. Unlike any of the other living species, man has succeeded both consciously and subconsciously in greatly altering his fundamental ecological patterning. None of the other living species have altered their ecological patterning. All the species other than man are distinguishable throughout geologic and biologic history by their approximately unaltered ecological patterning. In the last half century, man has graduated from a local twelve-mile radius daily domain into a world around multi-thousand-miles radius daily domain, as a consequence of his ability to alter his own ecological patterning.

I have for a third of a century been convinced that thoughts must be translated into patterns that can be articulated out of the organized capabilities of man and that these patterns, which can be translated from our thoughts into physical actions, then become utterly impersonal facilities that begin when adopted in emergencies to spontaneously and subconsciously change the relative advantage of man with respect to his total environment. It is a philosophic requirement of my comprehensive working hypotheses that the intellectually projected tools which result in new ecological patternings must give man consciously appreciable advantage increase. My experience shows that these impersonal tools tend to eliminate many of the errors of conceptioning that men who have not translated their thoughts into experimental physical undertakings have heretofore imposed upon one another as inherited *conventional* thoughts and misinterpretations of their respective experiences,—misconceptions which they have hopefully and lovingly gone on relaying for ages from one generation to the next.

I am convinced that humanity is characterized by extraordinary love for its new life and yet has been misinforming its new life to such an extent that the new life is continually at a greater disadvantage than it would be if abandoned in the wilderness by the parents. For an instance of misconception extension there is my own case. I was born in 1895. The airplane was invented when I was 9 years old. Up to the time I was 9 years old, the idea that man could fly was held to be preposterous, and anybody could tell you so. My own boyhood attempts to make flying machines were considered wasted time. I have lived deeply into the period when flying is no longer impossible, but nonetheless a period in which the supremely ruling social conventions and economic dogma have continued to presuppose a nonflying man ecology.

The Architect as World Planner.

(During the International Congress of Architects, held in London in July, 1961, *Architectural Design* asked Fuller to contribute his views on the role of the architect in the present world situation. An extract from his proposal for a "World Design Plan," to be implemented by architectural schools around the world, is given below.)

. . . I propose that the architectural departments of all the universities around the world be encouraged by the UIA [Union of International Architects] to invest the next ten years in a continuing problem of how to make the total world's resources serve 100 per cent of humanity through competent design.

The general theory of education at present starts students

off with elementary components and gradually increases the size of the complex of components with which the student will be concerned. The scheme is to go from the particular towards the whole but seems never to reach the whole. In many of the architectural schools the first-year student is given a problem in terms of a country town and has to plan and design the buildings for that country town. The next year he must do a larger town, a small industrial town. In the third year he is engaged in a large industrial city, and in his fourth year he is engaged with larger cities, such as London or New York. The schools never reach out to national let alone world problems. Local town planning is almost everywhere invalidated by the sweep of world events. The automobile highway cloverleaf programmes are inadequate to the concept of total man being advantaged with his own vehicle; parking problems continually frustrate and negate the too-local horizon of town planning.

The first year's total world planning by the students and its designed implementation may be expected to disclose great amateurishness and inadequacies, but not only will the criticism come from the architectural profession, but it will also be evoked from the politicos, from the economists, the industrialists, excited by its treading on their doorsteps, out of which criticism the next year's round of world designing by the students may be greatly advantaged. The second, third and fourth years should show swift acceleration in the comprehension of the problem and the degree of satisfaction of the problem.

The world planning by the students must be predicated upon the concept of first things first, upon a scheduled hierarchy of events.

The comprehensive world resources data now exist in a number of establishments, but is primarily available to all the universities of the world through UNESCO. What UNESCO does not have, it is in a good position to direct the researcher to successfully acquire.

At the present moment in history, what is spoken of as foreign policy by the respective nations consists essentially of their plans to bring about conditions which would uniquely foster their respective unique kinds of survival in the Malthusian "you or me-ness." For any one of the foreign policies of any of the nations or groups of nations to become a world plan, would mean that approximately one-half of the world's nations would have to surrender, and would mean the development of a highly biased plan as applied to the whole. In the nature of political compromises, it is logical to assume that the foreign policy of any one nation will never succeed in satisfying comprehensive world planning.

It is clearly manifest, however, in this Sixth Congress of the International Union of Architects that the architects are able to think regarding such world planning in a manner transcendental to any political bias. My experience around the world and amongst the students tells me that the students themselves tend always to transcend political bias and that all of them are concerned with the concept of making the world work through competent design.

In much investigation and inquiry I have had no negative response to the programme of organization of the student capability to the raising of the performance of the world resources to serve 100 per cent of humanity by peaceful, comprehensive laboratory experiment and progressive design evolution.

It is probable that if the architectural students are progressively disciplined to breadth of capability in chemistry, physics, mathematics, bio-chemistry, psychology, economics, and industrial technology, they will swiftly and ably penetrate the most advanced scientific minds resident in the university, and as their programmes evolve from year to year in improving capability, the students will be able to bring the highest integral scientific resources of man to bear upon their solutions of world town planning and its design instrumentation and operational regeneration.

The next Congress should then be almost completely preoccupied with reviewing all such inventories and plans— with this first stocktaking of what man has to do, and what he has to do it with! What will appear will unquestionably be world news of the first order, and not only world news but the news that men all around the earth have waited for. The common goals for all to work toward will be reduced from empty words to simple physical objectives.

Selected Bibliography

WRITINGS ABOUT R. BUCKMINSTER FULLER

MacLeish, Archibald, ". . . the Industry that Industry Missed," *Fortune* magazine, July, 1932, pp. 60–69. Discussion and illustration of the Dymaxion house.

"Fuller's House," *Fortune* magazine, April, 1946, pp. 167–70. Discussion and illustration of the Wichita house.

Marks, Robert, W., "Bucky Fuller's Dymaxion World," *Science Illustrated*, November, 1948, pp. 30–31.

"Geodesic Dome; Fuller's Spidery New Framing System," *Architectural Forum*, August, 1951, pp. 144–51.

DeKooning, Elaine, "Dymaxion Artist," *Art News*, September, 1952, pp. 14–17.

Marks, Robert W., "The Dymaxion World of Bucky Fuller," *Gentry*, Spring, 1953.

"Bucky Fuller Finds a Client; Young Henry Ford Translates the Geodesic Dome into Aluminum and Plastic," *Architectural Forum*, May, 1953, pp. 108–11. Discussion of the Ford Rotunda Dome.

"R. Buckminster Fuller; Ein Pionier des 20. Jahrhunderts," *Kontinente*, July-August, 1954, pp. 41–42. Article includes 23" x 40" sheet cut out of Dymaxion Map.

Lane, Colonel Henry C. (U.S.M.C., Head of Aviation Logistics and Material Branch H.Q., U.S.M.C.) "Study of Shelter Logistics," *Marine Corps Aviation, Final Report,* January, 1955. Discussion of use of geodesic domes.

"Cycle of Evolution; the Work of Buckminster Fuller," *Architectural Record*, June, 1955, pp. 155–62. Article includes five-hundred-word piece by Fuller.

"Bucky Fuller Builds an All Plastic Dome," *Architectural Record*, November, 1955, p. 235. Report on geodesic radome.

McHale, John, "Buckminster Fuller," *Architectural Review*, July, 1956, pp. 12–20.

Olson, Ken and Miller, Al, "A Bright New Hope for Low Cost Building!" *Better Homes and Gardens*, June, 1957, pp. 72–73.

Cort, David, "Darkness under the Dome," *Nation*, March 1, 1958, pp. 187–88.

McHale, John, "Total Design," *Architecture and Building*, July, 1958, pp. 244–51.

"Fuller Future," *Time* magazine, October 20, 1958, pp. 84–87.

Tomkins, Calvin, "Architecture: Umbrella Man," *Newsweek*, July 13, 1959, p. 84.

Marks, Robert W., "The Breakthrough of Buckminster Fuller," *New York Times Magazine*, August 23, 1959, p. 15.

McHale, John, "Fuller's Universal Requirements Checklist," *Architectural Design*, March, 1960, pp. 101–10.

McHale, John, "Richard Buckminster Fuller," *Architectural Design*, July, 1961, pp. 290–327. Article includes 7,000-word letter written to the author in 1955.

Book:

Marks, Robert W., *The Dymaxion World of Buckminster Fuller*. New York, Reinhold Publishing Corporation, 1960. A fully illustrated and documented book.

WRITINGS BY R. BUCKMINSTER FULLER

Articles:

"Universal Architecture," *Shelter Magazine*, February, 1932, pp. 22–25, 34–41, April, 1932, pp. 30–36.

"Fluid Geography," (first edition) *American Neptune*, April, 1944, pp. 119–36.

"Comprehensive Design 1," *Transformation*, Vol. I, 1950, pp. 18–23.

"Comprehensive Design 2," *Harvard Society Bulletin*, November, 1952.

"Industrial Logistics and Design Strategy," *The Pennsylvania Triangle*, University of Pennsylvania Engineering School Magazine, November, 1952, pp. 10–12, 24–25.

The Student Publication of the School of Design, North Carolina State College:

"The 90% Automatic Factory, Vol. II, No. 1, Fall, 1951, pp. 29–33.

"4D Timelock," Chapters 10, 11, 12, Vol. II, No. 3, Spring, 1952, pp. 11–20.

"The Architect and Agriculture," Vol. III, No. 1, Fall, 1952, pp. 15–19.

"Architecture from the Scientific Viewpoint," Vol. III, No. 3, Spring, 1953, pp. 6–9.

"No More Second Hand God," Vol. IV, No. 1, Fall, 1953, pp. 16–24.

"Fluid Geography," (second edition), Vol. IV, No. 2, Winter, 1954, pp. 41–48.

"Considerations for a Curriculum," Vol. IV, No. 3, Winter, 1954, pp. 14–18.

"The Textile Mill of Tomorrow," *American Fabrics*, Spring, 1953, pp. 100–103.

"Architecture Out of the Laboratory," *Dimension* (Student publication of the College of Architecture and Design, University of Michigan), Vol. I, No. 1, Spring, 1955.

124   "The R.I.B.A. Discourse, 1958; Experimental Probing of Architectural Initiative," *Royal Institute of British Architects Journal*, October, 1958, pp. 415–24.

"The Comprehensive Man," *Northwest Review*, Spring, 1959, pp. 23–55.

"A Philosophy of Space and Shape," *Consulting Engineer*, December, 1959.

"Universal Requirements of a Dwelling Advantage," *Architectural Design*, March, 1960, pp. 101–10.

"Prime Design," *Bennington College Bulletin*, May, 1960.

"Isamu Noguchi," *Palette*, Magazine of Connecticut Arts Association, Winter, 1960.

"The Architect as World Planner," *Architectural Design*, August, 1961, p. 235.

"Tensegrity," *Portfolio and Art News Annual*, No. 4, 1961, pp. 112–27, 148. Introduction by John McHale.

Books:

Nine Chains to the Moon. New York, J. B. Lippincott Co., 1938.

With L. Babcock, *New Worlds in Engineering.* New York, Chrysler Corporation, 1940.

Quadrat Print—Buckminster Fuller, P. Brattinga, ed., (in four languages). Hilversum, Netherlands, Strendrukkerij de Jong & Co., Summer, 1958.

Education Automation. Carbondale, Southern Illinois University Press, 1962.

No More Second Hand God. Carbondale, Southern Illinois University Press, 1962.

Index

Numbers in regular roman type refer to text pages; *italic* figures refer to the plates.

Illustration Credits

All photographs appear with the kind permission of R. Buckminster Fuller, Carbondale, Illinois.

The following photographs were supplied through the courtesy of Leco Photo Service, New York City: 1, 2, 3, 4, 5, 6, 7, 8, 10, 11, 13, 15, 16, 17, 18, 19, 20, 21, 23, 24, 25, 27, 29, 30, 31, 32, 33, 38, 39, 41, 42, 44, 45, 46, 47, 48, 49, 50, 51, 52, 53, 54, 55, 56, 57, 58, 59, 60, 61, 62, 63, 64, 65, 67, 68, 69, 70, 71, 72, 73, 74, 75, 77, 78, 79, 80, 81, 82, 84, 85, 86, 87, 88, 89, 90, 91, 92, 93, 94, 96, 97, 98, 99, 100, 102, 103.

Hedrich-Blessing, Chicago, for *Fortune:* 28

Courtesy of the Museum of Modern Art, New York: 43, 83 (photo by Alexandre Georges)

Pease Woodwork Company, Hamilton, Ohio: 76

Union Tank Car Company, Chicago: 95

Text printed in offset by Murray Printing Company, Forge Village, Massachusetts; illustrations in Pictone offset by Pictorial Offset, New York City. Set in Bodoni Book with Inserat Grotesk. Bound by The Haddon Craftsmen, Scranton, Pennsylvania. Format by Lustig & Reich.